W9-CKA-514

Lion House

Entertaining

Lion House Entertaining

**EAGLE
GATE**

SALT LAKE CITY, UTAH

Also available from Deseret Book:

Lion House Recipes

Christmas Recipes from the Lion House

Lion House International Recipes

Lion House Desserts

© 2001 Hotel Temple Square Corporation

All rights reserved. No part of this book may be reproduced in any form or by any means without permission in writing from the publisher, Deseret Book Company, P. O. Box 30178, Salt Lake City, Utah 84130. This work is not an official publication of The Church of Jesus Christ of Latter-day Saints. The views expressed herein are the responsibility of the author and do not necessarily represent the position of the Church or of Deseret Book Company.

Eagle Gate is a registered trademark of Deseret Book Company.

Visit us at www.deseretbook.com

Library of Congress Cataloging-in-Publication Data

Lion House entertaining.
    p.   cm.
Includes index.
ISBN 1-57345-971-2
1. Cookery, American.   2. Lion House (Restaurant)   3. Entertaining.   I. Eagle Gate.
TX715 .L7594 2002
641.5973—dc21   2001004779

Printed in the United States of America   42316-6824
Inland Press, Menomonee Falls, WI

10 9 8 7 6 5 4 3 2 1

Contents

Acknowledgments

Hotel Temple Square Corporation would like to thank the many people involved in the creation of this book.

We would like to thank all those at the Lion House who helped with this project, including those who wrote and tested the recipes and those who prepared the food for the photo shoots. Special thanks goes to Geri Tiedemann, Julie Ulrich, Brenda Hopkin, Ann Sudweeks, Alba Marroquin, Julie Gardner, and Barbara Carling.

Thanks goes to many people at Deseret Book, including Jana Erickson for the concept and her many hours of work to see it to fruition, Jennifer Adams for the editing, Shauna Gibby for the design, and Tonya Facemyer for the typesetting.

We would like to thank John Luke for the photography. Additional photos by Russell Winegar. Thanks to Maxine Bramwell for the food styling.

We also express thanks to the following individuals and companies that loaned us their dishes and linens for the photographs: Maxine Bramwell, Laurie Cook, Rebecca Crookston, Jana Erickson, Shauna Gibby, Diane Harding, Dianna Hymas, Sheryl Roderick, Elizabeth Van Roosendaal, The Basket Loft, Gentler Times, and Meier and Frank.

The floral arrangements were by Jolene Campbell at Perfect Petals and Colleen Hanson with the Joseph Smith Memorial Building Floral Department.

Illustrations for the napkin folding were created by Sheryl Roderick and Shauna Gibby. The cover lettering was created by James Fedor.

The Lion House at Christmastime. William Ward, the young English artist who sculpted the lion that graces the doorway, also created the eagle that sits above Eagle Gate.

Introduction to the Lion House

1

The historic Lion House was built from 1855 to 1856 by the great Mormon pioneer leader and colonizer, Brigham Young. For two decades this fine pioneer structure was filled to overflowing with the abundant family of its builder and owner. Located next door to the Beehive House, which served as Brigham's official residence, the Lion House was built as a home for many of his wives and children. Here he held receptions for great men of the world, made plans that helped determine the future of the struggling Utah territory, and conducted family activities in love and harmony.

The building was designed by Truman O. Angell, architect of the Salt Lake Temple and brother of Brigham's second wife, Mary Ann Angell. The Lion House was built with native sandstone, possibly from nearby City Creek Canyon, and covered with cream-colored adobe. The distinctive exterior with its gabled windows, green shutters, and white woodwork resembles English architecture of the mid-1800s.

A commanding 1200-pound stone sculpture of a crouching lion, created by English craftsman William Ward, is mounted above the entrance and gives the mansion the name by which it is known

The built-in cupboards, behind and to the right of the Victorian-style Christmas tree, are original to the front parlor. Disguised by floor-to-ceiling wood doors, they were used to store household supplies. Elegant gold-trimmed china from Brigham Young's personal collection graces the dining table.

A built-in mirrored shelf was designed as part of the original front parlor to display some of Brigham Young's most treasured possessions.

Making taffy was a favorite activity for the Young family. The large steel hooks next to the fireplace on the lower level were installed so hot molasses could be strung and pulled into taffy. This room is now part of the Lion House Pantry.

around the world. Interestingly, Brigham Young was often called "The Lion of the Lord," which may have inspired the sculptor's work.

Originally the Lion House was a three-story home. Life revolved around the large front parlor located on the west side of the middle floor, just inside the massive paneled door which serves as the home's entrance. This parlor was known as "the prayer room" because Brigham Young would gather his family and guests here each evening at seven o'clock for prayers, hymn singing, and family counsel. Tradition holds that Brigham would ring a heavy, handheld bell three times to announce that the appointed hour was at hand, and all who could hear the bell were expected to attend.

Beyond the front parlor, a corridor divided the entire length of the main floor with staircases positioned at either end. Ten bedroom/sitting rooms were located on either side of the hallway, including the room where Brigham Young died on August 29, 1877.

The lower level of the Lion House bustled with the many domestic activities of pioneer family life. A long dining room filled much of the space and accommodated 50 to 70 people for daily meals. A typical breakfast might have included fresh eggs and toast with milk and fruit, or perhaps thick buckwheat cakes dripping with maple syrup. The noon meal was the largest meal of the day. Dinner, as it was called, consisted of meat, poultry, or fish, and an abundance of seasonal vegetables. Pies brimming with apples, squash, currants, gooseberries, plums, custard, or cranberries were often served as dessert following this meal. The evening meal, or supper, was light and usually consisted of mush or hominy accompanied by bread, cheese, and fruit.

A kitchen and buttery (or pantry), were essential to the massive food preparation required for so many people, as was a cellar for storing fruits, vegetables, and milk. A laundry room, weaving room, and school room were also located on this floor.

The upper level of the home consisted of twenty small dormitory-style bedrooms, each outfitted with a small Lady Franklin stove, a wardrobe, and a specified number of beds depending on the size of the room. Gabled windows provided a view of the nearby temple grounds to the west and the Beehive House, framed by the beautiful Wasatch Mountains, to the east.

Following Brigham Young's death, each remaining wife was provided with a home of her own or was guaranteed living quarters at the Lion House for the remainder of her life.

In the early 1900s, the home was sold to The Church of Jesus Christ of Latter-day Saints and was used for various educational, social, and community activities.

The Lion House underwent an extensive renovation from 1963 to 1968, after which it was reopened as a social center. The elegance and beauty of the Victorian period in which it was built has been diligently preserved. Much of the original interior woodwork still exists. This pine woodwork was carefully "grained," or painted, by skilled pioneer craftsmen to resemble beautiful hardwoods such as mahogany, oak, and maple that were unavailable to Brigham Young when the home was built.

During the renovation, new draperies were fashioned from damask, mohair, and dimity fabrics typical of the mid-1800s. Carpets were painstakingly reproduced using original swatches of authentic pioneer carpets. Some of the original furnishings in the home were preserved, while numerous antiques that reflect the decor of the Victorian period were acquired to complement the existing pieces.

Many of the original bedroom walls were removed during an extensive renovation from 1963 to 1968 in order to provide larger entertaining rooms for the present-day Lion House. This beautiful handcrafted staircase, adorned with garlands and poinsettias for Christmas, stands where Brigham Young's bedroom was originally.

The courtyard and garden area. The pleasant garden atmosphere makes this a favorite spot for outdoor wedding receptions and luncheons.

The banquet room is the site of many festive holiday events. The red-and-white transferware dishes have been a hallmark of the Lion House for many years.

With the exception of the front parlor, the interior has been modified to provide ample room for dining and entertaining. The main floor holds the front parlor, the 1875 room, the social room, the pioneer room, and the garden room. A children's party room is also located on the main floor. Here children can participate in pioneer traditions as they celebrate birthdays and other special occasions.

A charming courtyard and garden connect the east side of the Lion House to the Beehive House. During the spring and summer months, this is a popular location for weddings, luncheons, and restaurant dining.

The upper floor was altered to create three large dining rooms known as the banquet room, the gable room, and the buffet room. These rooms now serve the majority of dining guests for catered events at the Lion House.

The lower floor now houses the Lion House Pantry, a cafeteria-style restaurant that offers tempting home-cooked food, primarily for lunch guests.

In 1964 the Lion House was declared a national historic landmark. Today it continues to represent the culture and beauty of its pioneer heritage. A favorite place for receptions, dinners, wedding parties, luncheons, and meetings, the Lion House remains a tangible link of the present with the past.

Handmade quilts and vintage china contribute to the homey atmosphere of the Lion House Pantry.

Antique dolls and toys fill the corner cabinet in the Children's Room. Party guests are treated to pioneer stories, games, and taffy pulling.

Entertaining is an opportunity to express individual
personality and style.

2

Simply put, entertaining should be pleasurable—a harmonious blending of wonderful food, an inviting setting, and people you care about. Celebrations should be fun for everyone, including the hosts. Following a few simple guidelines will help make an event memorable and enjoyable for you and your guests.

SIMPLE GUIDELINES

First, do what you enjoy. Take your inspiration from anything that is unique and special to you or your family. If you are a great gardener, give an outdoor party when your plants are in full bloom. If the kitchen is your favorite room in the house, plan a party where guests are invited to help prepare the food and serve it directly from the stove. If someone in your family plays an instrument, hold a recital or a Christmas carol party featuring your star performer. You can make any event uniquely yours by adding your own creative touch.

Next, keep it manageable and work with what you have. If you don't have room for a sit-down dinner for twenty guests, plan a buffet instead. Entertaining can be successful on a large or small budget. Define the scope of the event to help you concentrate on the most important elements, then focus on what you like to do. If you love to

Formal sit-down dinners are an excellent way to bring together family and friends.

Dinner buffets lend themselves to large guest lists and can offer formal foods in a more casual setting.

PAN SIZES AND SUBSTITUTIONS

9-inch springform pan = 9-inch square pan

9-inch round = 8-inch square pan

9x5-inch loaf = 9-inch square pan

12-cup bundt cake = 10x4-inch angel food cake pan

1-quart casserole = 9-inch pie pan

1½-quart casserole = 8-inch square pan

2-quart casserole = 9-inch square pan

3-quart casserole = 13x9-inch rectangular pan

cook, recruit someone else to do the cleaning. If you enjoy decorating more than spending time in the kitchen, use your creative skills to make a spectacular presentation of simpler menu items.

Last of all, be flexible. There is no such thing as a "perfect" party where every detail comes off without a flaw. Experienced hosts know to expect the unexpected. The more prepared you are, the better you will be able to handle the unexpected with a smile. Even mistakes can make for a memorable party, so focus on helping your guests feel comfortable and relaxed, and they are certain to appreciate your efforts.

WHAT'S IN THIS BOOK

This book is a collection of menus and recipes for many occasions. Of course, most of the menus will work well for other events as well. Mix and match the recipes according to your specific event and tastes. Menus can also be used as a springboard for your own ideas. However you decide to entertain, the following suggestions will help you plan and present a successful event—one that is as extravagant or as simple as you wish.

ORGANIZING

The key to successful entertaining is preparation. It is just as important to plan well for three guests as it is for thirty. The more time and effort you put into preparation, the more relaxed and smooth-flowing the party will be. And the more tasks you can actually complete beforehand, the lighter your workload will be on the day of the party.

Planning and list-making go hand-in-hand. The following suggestions may be helpful when you are planning your event.

• A well-built menu should allow you to prepare some dishes in advance. You may want to include a few items that are simple to prepare and a few others that may take a little more effort but will dazzle your guests. Consider any special preferences or dietary requirements of your guests as you are planning. You may also want to consider what produce is in season. Finalize your menu on paper and collect all the recipes you will need.

- Use the menu to make a list of every ingredient you will need to buy and how much of each item is needed. Be sure to include drinks, paper goods, and decorations. Do your shopping as far in advance as possible.

- Read the entire recipe for each dish and make a time line of what will be prepared when. It is helpful to combine similar chores for multiple recipes, especially when cooking for company. For example, if more than one recipe calls for chopped onions, chop the entire quantity in one step and divide it into separate plastic bags, labeled by the recipe or proportion. Think of preparing a meal as being like conducting an orchestra. Not all of the instruments will be playing at the same time. So while you are waiting for a pot of water to come to a boil, you can be grating cheese for one recipe or washing vegetables for another.

- For large events with many menu items, it can be helpful to make a list of which plates, platters, and utensils will be used to serve each dish. If you plan to use kitchen help, affix sticky notes to drawers and cabinets to show helpers exactly where to find each piece.

- Have all ingredients ready to use—washed, chopped, measured, etc.— before you begin preparing each dish. Much of the preliminary work can be done well in advance of the event to cut down on actual cooking time.

- Decide in advance what to do with leftovers. Keep plenty of plastic containers and self-sealing plastic bags on hand, as well as plastic wrap and foil.

- Keep all your lists, recipes, and notes in a file folder or notebook, or electronically, for future reference.

EQUIVALENCY CHART

LIQUID MEASURES
1 gal = 4 qt = 8 pt = 16 cups = 128 fl oz
½ gal = 2 qt = 4 pt = 8 cups = 64 fl oz
¼ gal = 1 qt = 2 pt = 4 cups = 32 fl oz
½ qt = 1 pt = 2 cups = 16 fl oz
¼ qt = ½ pt = 1 cup = 8 fl oz

DRY MEASURES
1 cup = 16 Tbsp = 48 tsp = 250mL
¾ cup = 12 Tbsp = 36 tsp = 175mL
⅔ cup = 10⅓ Tbsp = 32 tsp = 150mL
½ cup = 8 Tbsp = 24 tsp = 125mL
⅓ cup = 5⅓ Tbsp = 16 tsp = 75mL
¼ cup = 4 Tbsp = 12 tsp = 50mL
⅛ cup = 2 Tbsp = 6 tsp = 30mL
1 Tbsp = 3 tsp = 15mL

SETTING THE SCENE

The specifics of an event will often determine the form your entertaining will take. They can also determine where the event will be held. The dining room is the obvious place to start, but depending upon the number of guests, the occasion, and the time of year, you could just as easily set a table by the fireplace or dine out-of-doors. With some creative planning, entertaining at home can offer a variety of possibilities. If more space is needed, consider seating in the living room, family room, a hall foyer, or a combination of rooms. Perhaps there are rooms that can be rearranged to better accommodate the number of guests and your plans.

The arrangement of tables is equally flexible. Any shape, size, and configuration of tables can work, although each place setting should be at least twenty-four inches wide and eighteen inches deep for comfortable dining. If you need to seat a crowd larger than a traditional dining-room table will accommodate, consider a U-shaped formation with an existing rectangular dining room table and two folding tables positioned perpendicularly on each end. And remember that it is not necessary to fit everyone at one table; two tables may be better than one.

TABLE SETTINGS

Setting a table is like painting on a canvas. Every detail is important, and every element helps complete the picture. The colors, patterns, textures, and shapes that you select determine the mood of the finished piece. An atmosphere that is warm and sunny, soft and romantic, or rich and vibrant can be achieved by the mix of linens, plates, glassware, and decorations you choose. Always keep in mind, however, that the food is the most important thing and that your table settings and decorations should complement rather than disguise it.

For special events, set the table the day or night before. This simple rule

Delicate china and conservative linens create a pleasant, semiformal dining atmosphere.

can help you feel more relaxed on the day of your party and will also give you an opportunity to focus on the mood you want to create with the table settings and decorations. In addition, setting the table in advance serves as a check to make sure you have everything you need.

LINENS

Before setting your table, you will need to select a tablecloth or place mats. What goes on the table depends on your individual style and the type of event you are hosting. In general, a table can be minimally set with only the place settings. However, a beautifully set table can help create a festive mood and make your guests feel important. If space is limited, forego using place mats—which can make a table look too cluttered—and use a runner instead. A runner looks best when it either drapes off the table like a tablecloth or is somewhat shorter than the length of the table. Runners can also be substituted for place mats when placed on both sides of a table, or two runners can be crisscrossed to form an X in the center of a rectangular table.

Be creative and consider a nontraditional table covering such as a rug, quilt, bedspread, or sheet. For a dramatic effect, place a white lace topper over a dark, richly colored cloth. As a general rule, more formal tables require longer tablecloths, ideally twelve to sixteen inches on each side. Save floor-length cloths for buffet tables or to disguise card table legs. To avoid a skimpy look, make sure the cloth has at least a nine-inch drop from each edge.

For shapes and sizes of cloths to fit your table, as well as the number of guests that can be comfortably seated at different-sized tables, see the tablecloth size chart to the right.

Choose easy-to-clean cloths that require minimal ironing. Be sure to have the tablecloth and napkins laundered and pressed well in advance of the event.

TABLECLOTH SIZE CHART

SQUARE
Table size 28" to 40"
Cloth size 52" x 52"
Seats 4 people

ROUND
Table size 30" to 42" diameter
Cloth size 52" round
Seats 4 people

Table size 42" to 44" diameter
Cloth size 60" to 68"
Seats 4 to 6 people

Table size 42" to 54" diameter
Cloth size 68" w/fringe
Seats 6 people

Table size 42" to 60" diameter
Cloth size 72" round
Seats 6 people

Table size 64" to 76" diameter
Cloth size 90" round
Seats 6 to 8 people

OBLONG
Table size 28" x 46" to 36" x 54"
Cloth size 52" x 70"
Seats 4 to 6 people

Table size 36" x 56" to 42" x 62"
Cloth size 60" x 80"
Seats 6 to 8 people

Table size 42" x 60" to 48" x 72"
Cloth size 72" x 90"
Seats 6 to 8 people

Table size 42" x 72" to 48" x 90"
Cloth size 72" x 108"
Seats 8 to 10 people

OVAL
Table size 28" x 46" to 36" x 54"
Cloth size 52" x 70"
Seats 4 to 6 people

Table size 36" x 56" to 42" x 62"
Cloth size 60" x 80"
Seats 6 to 8 people

Table size 42" x 60" to 48" x 72"
Cloth size 72" x 90"
Seats 6 to 8 people

Table size 42" x 72" to 48" x 90"
Cloth size 72" x 108"
Seats 8 to 10 people

You can dress up a simple dinner by adding an unusual salad or homemade dessert.

NAPKINS

Napkins should coordinate with the rest of the table setting, but they don't necessarily have to be part of a matched set. Napkins can help create a mood—by the fabric, by the way they are folded, and by the way they are placed on the table. Typically square in shape, napkins should be generously sized (a minimum of sixteen inches). Napkin rings, which were once purely practical and used to identify a family member's personal napkin between launderings, are now simply decorative and completely optional. To dress up a napkin without a napkin ring, tie it with raffia or wire-edged ribbon, or tuck in a flower. Setting a sprig of fragrant rosemary, the traditional token of love and remembrance, on each napkin also adds a welcoming touch.

NAPKIN FOLDING

During the seventeenth century, the art of napkin folding was a respected and well-paid profession with strict and detailed rules. Today, the only rules that apply to napkin folding are those of common sense. Remember that overly fancy flourishes can complicate the serving of food. For instance, a napkin bursting from a goblet may look spectacular, but it means that no water can be poured until the guests are seated with the napkins in their laps. This is fine for the very special occasion; however, it is generally safest to position napkins to the left of the place setting or directly on a plate. For casual events or buffet tables, napkins can be rolled and placed in a container or stacked neatly at the end of the table.

TWELVE EASY WAYS TO FOLD A NAPKIN

The following methods for napkin folding range from the simple to the complicated. Practice your hand at different styles to find the perfect match for your occasion.

1. Simple Triangle. Fold napkin in half to form a triangle with point down. Pick up napkin from the center of the folded side and pull through napkin ring. As a variation, use two napkins of different colors. Lay the top napkin on the bottom napkin at an angle, so that the corners of the top napkin are between the corners of the bottom napkin before folding in half.

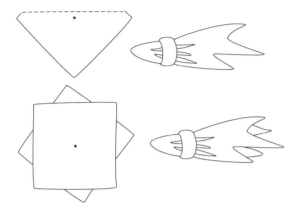

2. Simple Roll. Fold napkin in half to form a rectangle. Roll napkin into a log and slide through napkin ring or tie with ribbon.

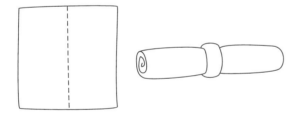

3. The Diamond. Position flat napkin in a diamond shape. Accordian pleat the left and right corners toward the center of the cloth, until the folds meet. Fold the napkin in half by bringing the bottom corner up to the top corner. Slide the folded bottom edge through the napkin ring.

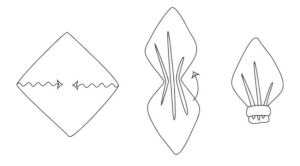

An easy-to-make but elegant lunch is perfect for a birthday party, bridal shower, or get-together with friends.

COOKING TERMS

baste: to moisten meat by spooning, brushing, or squirting a liquid, such as meat drippings, stock, or butter over the meat while it cooks.

beat: to mix by stirring, either by hand or with an electric mixer.

blanch: to prepare fruits and vegetables by immersing in boiling water. This may also help to loosen the skins of such fruits as tomatoes and peaches.

blend: to combine separate ingredients, such as oil, vinegar, and seasonings, until they are uniformly mixed.

braise: to cook meat or vegetables by browning in butter or oil and then cooking further in a covered pot with a small amount of liquid over medium or low heat.

broil: to cook by direct exposure to dry heat in an oven set on broil. Broiling can be a low-fat way to cook because it does not require oil or butter.

brown: to cook meat or vegetables until the outside is brown in color.

chop: to cut in small pieces with a knife or food processor.

cream: to blend ingredients such as butter, margarine, or shortening to the consistency of a light and fluffy cream.

cube: to cut into uniform ½-inch square shapes.

cut in: to mix a solid fat, such as butter, with a dry ingredient, such as flour, until the mixture forms small particles. This is often done with a pastry blender.

dice: to cut into small, uniform ¼-inch pieces.

dissolve: to combine a liquid and a solid until they are one mixture and the solid is liquefied, as in dissolving gelatin in water.

fold: to incorporate a lighter ingredient into a heavier mixture by bringing the bottom of the mixture to the top without stirring or beating.

grate: to reduce a food to small particles by rubbing over a rough grating surface, as to grate cheese.

grill: to cook on a series of connected parallel metal bars over hot coals or a fire, usually outdoors.

4. The Tie. Fold napkin in half to form a triangle with point down. Fold left and right corners of triangle toward center back, overlapping a few inches. Gather sides and slide napkin ring over top edge. As a variation, tie a ribbon around the folded napkin approximately two inches from top edge.

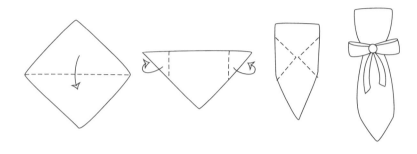

5. The Party Fan. Accordian-fold flat napkin into one-inch pleats. Fold pleated napkin in half and slide napkin ring over folded point, causing pleats to fan out. For a smaller fan that can stand upright, fold side edges of square napkin to center, creating a tall rectangle. Pull out top center corners to outside folded edges of napkin. From top, roll napkin tightly towards center. Holding rolled section, accordian-pleat the bottom half of napkin toward center. Fold roll and pleats in half with the pleats on the outside of the fold. Slide napkin ring through folded point and set upright.

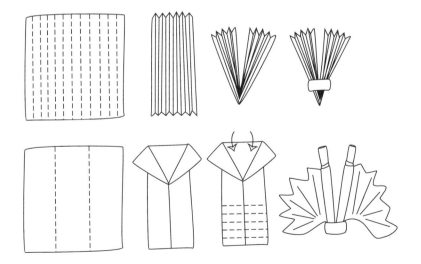

6. The Crown. Fold napkin in half with folded edge at bottom. Fold bottom left corner up to top center. Fold top right corner down to bottom center. Turn napkin over and fold entire bottom edge up to top edge. Hold top center edge of napkin and lift slightly so that the two folded points fall free. Fold over the left *side* corner slightly past center, using the *bottom* left corner as a midpoint for the new fold, and tuck under right flap. Fold right *side* corner behind napkin, using *bottom* right corner as a midpoint for the new fold, and tuck in. Turn napkin so points are upright and stand on center of plate.

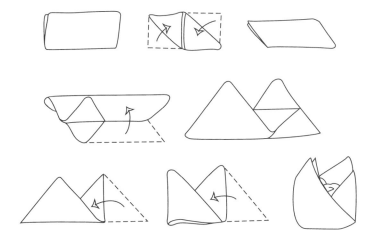

7. Bonaparte. Fold napkin in half to form a triangle with point at top. Fold left and right corners up to the top corner forming a diamond shape. Fold bottom corner up to one inch below top corner. Turn and place folded edge to left of place setting.

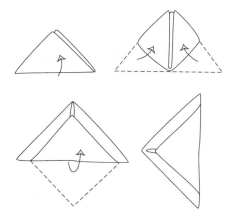

knead: to mix and work dough manually or with an electric mixer until smooth and elastic in order to release the gluten in the yeast. To knead manually, press dough with the heels of the hands, fold in half, turn dough a quarter turn, and repeat until smooth.

marinate: to put meats or vegetables in a mixture—usually made of oil, vinegar, or lemon juice and seasonings—to flavor and tenderize.

mince: to cut or chop into very small, irregularly shaped pieces.

parboil: to boil briefly as a preliminary or incomplete cooking procedure

puree: to liquefy or mash a solid food into a thick, smooth consistency, usually in a blender or food processor.

roast: to cook in an oven using dry heat, usually without liquid.

sauté: to fry ingredients in a small amount of fat until softened or browned.

score: to make shallow cuts into the surface of a meat to aid marinade absorption, to help tenderize, and to decorate.

shred: to separate or tear into small, thin, irregular pieces.

sift: to separate dry ingredients through a sieve or sifter to incorporate air and eliminate lumps.

simmer: to cook food in liquid over low heat so tiny bubbles just break the surface.

steam: to cook over boiling water using a steamer basket or a special steamer pot.

stir: to mix ingredients together manually using a circular movement.

stir-fry: to cook quickly over high heat in a lightly oiled pan while stirring continuously.

sweat: to cook slowly over low heat in butter, usually covered, without browning.

toss: to mix lightly with a repeated, gentle, lifting motion until well coated with a dressing or until the elements are thoroughly combined.

whip: to beat ingredients rapidly into a froth with a whisk or electric mixer to incorporate air and increase volume.

Napkins of different fabrics and sizes work well in the candle fold and make an attractive display as part of the table centerpiece.

8. Ascot Tie. Fold napkin in half to form a triangle with point at top. Fold bottom edge up one quarter heighth of napkin (approximately two inches). Fold up again one quarter heighth of napkin. Fold right corner across napkin halfway between the top and left corners, extending point several inches beyond the left side of the napkin. Repeat with left corner. Turn napkin over and place in center of plate.

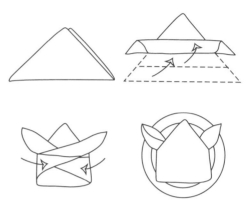

9. The Candle. Fold napkin in half to form a triangle with point at top. Fold bottom edge up one inch. Turn napkin over. Beginning at the left corner, tightly roll napkin into a cylinder shape. Tuck right corner into bottom folded edge and stand napkin upright.

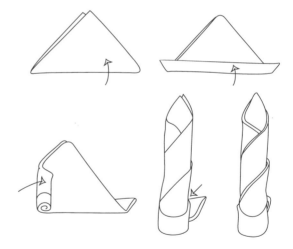

10. Muldevan Fold. Fold napkin in half to form a triangle with point at bottom. Fold right corner down to bottom corner. Repeat with left corner to form a diamond shape. Fold bottom half of napkin under, bringing bottom corner behind top corner and forming a triangle. Fold right side of napkin behind

left side. Turn folded napkin so that it stands on its longest side. Position in center of plate.

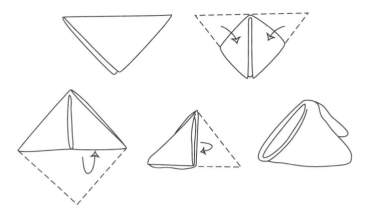

11. Buffet Pocket Fold. Fold napkin in quarters and position in a diamond shape with open edges on either side of the top half. Fold down top two edges of upper corner, almost meeting the bottom corner. Fold the right and left corners behind the napkin so that they overlap a couple of inches at the back. Place flatware or party favor inside the pocket.

Buffet pocket fold napkins are a fun and easy way to keep napkins and silverware together for guests in a buffet-style dining setting.

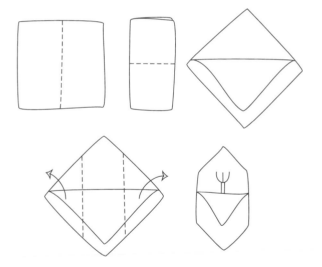

12. Fleur-de-Lys. Fold napkin in half to form a triangle with point at top. Fold left and right corners up to top point forming a diamond. Bring bottom point up to within one inch of top point, then fold that same point back down to center bottom edge. Fold left and right corners back behind napkin, tucking

Apples
I medium apple = I cup chopped or
1½ cups thinly sliced

Asparagus
16 to 20 stalks = I pound

Bacon
8 slices, crisply cooked = ½ cup
crumbled

Bread
1½ slices = I cup soft cubes
4 to 5 slices, dried = I cup dry
crumbs

Broccoli
2 cups florets = 6 ounces

Butter, margarine, or spread
I stick = ½ cup

Carrots
2 medium = I cup ¼-inch slices

Celery
2 medium stalks = I cup, chopped or
thinly sliced

Cheese
4 ounces blue, cheddar, feta,
mozzarella, or Swiss = I cup
shredded
8 ounces cream cheese = I cup
16 ounces ricotta cheese = 2 cups

Chocolate
6 ounces of chips = I cup
I ounce unsweetened or semisweet
baking = I square or bar

Cream
8 ounces sour cream = I cup
½ pint whipping cream = I cup
(2 cups whipped)

Garlic
I medium clove = ½ teaspoon finely
chopped

Graham cracker crumbs
20 squares = 1½ cups

Lemon or Lime
I medium = 2 to 3 tablespoons juice
or 1½ to 3 teaspoons grated peel

Lettuce (iceberg or romaine)
I medium = 2 cups shredded or 9
cups bite-size pieces

left corner into right corner. Fold down top front points on each side, tucking points down into folded cuff. Stand upright on plate.

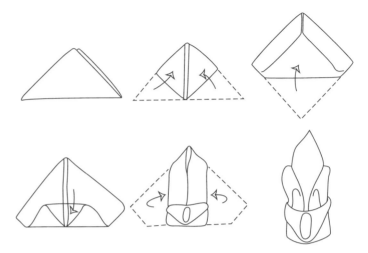

CENTERPIECES

The centerpiece of your table can nicely tie everything together and is a great way to show off the theme of your party. Be creative, but remember not to overdo it. The centerpiece should never distract from the rest of the table, and the table should never feel crowded because of the centerpiece.

Flowers and candles always make lovely centerpieces. Just be careful that they are not so bulky or tall that they inhibit conversation among your guests. Every season offers its own range of colorful flowers, leaves, and berries to arrange in a traditional bouquet, scatter naturally around candles in the center of the table, float in a shallow decorative bowl, or use individually as part of each place setting. If possible, choose flowers that complement your tableware and look for variety of sizes and textures. For very long tables, consider two vases of long-stemmed flowers, above eye level, placed at opposite ends of the table.

An unusual object that has special meaning to you or your family can also be used as a centerpiece. It will make a great conversation piece for your table and can be incorporated into your table design by surrounding it with greens, flowers, or ribbon.

A tabletop of gently flickering candlelight is both romantic and flattering to guests and place settings. Candles can be used in varying heights and widths, but keep lit candles either lower or higher than eye level so the flame does not distract your guests. Back up the candles with dim lamplight and turn off overhead lighting. Remember, never leave a lit candle unattended.

For crowded tables, an arrangement can be placed above a table instead of on it. Consider draping fresh greens on a chandelier, or hanging Christmas balls or hollow Easter eggs from the ceiling with transparent fishing line.

PLACE SETTINGS

A basic place setting consists of a dinner plate, salad plate, bread and butter plate, appropriate flatware for the meal, and a water glass. More elaborate meals may also include a soup bowl, dessert plate, milk glass, or juice glass. The dinner plate is the focal point of the setting.

Flatware is placed on the table, starting from the outside of the place setting, in the order each piece will be needed. Knives are placed to the right of the dinner plate with the cutting edge towards the plate. Spoons should be placed to the right of the knife. Place the dinner fork to the left of the plate, with the salad fork to the far left. (The exception to this rule would be if the salad is to be eaten with the main course. In that case, place the salad fork next to the plate and move the dinner fork to the outside position.)

Arrange the flatware handles in an even line with the edge of the plate. Flatware for dessert may be placed above the plate with the handle pointing toward the water glass, or it may be brought to the table at the same time dessert is served.

The salad plate is placed above the dinner fork unless a bread and butter plate is used. If both plates are needed, place the bread and butter plate above

Mushrooms, fresh
  8 ounces = 3 cups sliced
Olives, ripe pitted
  32 medium = 1 cup sliced
Onions
  2 medium green onions, with tops =
    2 tablespoons chopped
  4 medium green onions, with tops =
    ½ cup sliced
  1 medium yellow or white onion - ½
    cup chopped
Orange
  1 medium = 1 to 2 tablespoons
    grated peel or ⅓ to ½ cup juice
Peppers, bell
  1 small = ½ chopped
  1 medium = 1 cup chopped
  1 large = 1½ cup chopped
Potatoes
  3 medium red or white potatoes = 1
    pound
  10 to 12 small new potatoes = 1½
    pounds
  3 medium sweet potatoes or yams =
    1 pound
Rice, regular long-grain
  1 cup uncooked = 3 cups cooked
Sugar
  1 pound brown sugar = 2¼ cups
    packed
  1 pound granulated sugar = 2¼ cups
  1 pound powdered sugar = 4 cups
Tomatoes
  1 small = ½ cup chopped
  1 medium = ¾ cup chopped
  1 large = 1 cup chopped

the dinner fork and position the salad plate below and to the left. Or the salad plate may be placed on top of the dinner plate if the salad will be served as a first course. If space is a consideration and the table appears too crowded with both a salad plate and a bread and butter plate, it is best to omit the bread and butter plate.

Place the water glass at or near the tip of the dinner knife. If milk glasses are used, place the glass slightly lower and to the right of the water glass. On a very formal table, a juice glass might be served on a small plate at the center of the place setting. Otherwise, place the juice glass a little closer to the edge of the table from the last glass.

SERVING THE FOOD

There are several correct methods of serving food. Choose the method that best suits the arrangement and setting of your particular event.

Buffet style service from a nearby table or sideboard is convenient for large groups of people and can be used whether guests will be standing or seated. For a traditional sit-down meal, a buffet style can still be used to eliminate the clutter of serving dishes on the table or to avoid the more formal serving of previously prepared individual plates.

Plate service, where the plates are composed in the kitchen and served to the seated guests, is popular for large groups and allows the entree to be arranged decoratively on the plate. However, this often requires additional help. For a formal occasion with plated service, it is appropriate for a family member to wait on the table. For large groups, it may be helpful to use a nearby buffet table or serving cart to help facilitate the service.

For less formal events with fewer guests, one or more members of the group may assist with the serving and removal of dishes. Family or country style service, where serving dishes are placed in intervals on the table, is a good

The Fleur-de-Lys napkin fold adds drama to your place setting.

choice for casual events of up to eight or ten people.

When serving and removing dishes from the table, common-sense rules apply. Glassware and flatware on the right side of the place setting should be served and removed with the right hand. The bread and butter plate, the salad plate, and the dinner plate, along with any remaining flatware on the left side of the place setting, should be served and removed with the left hand and then transferred to the right hand for handling. Glasses should be refilled or removed from the right side.

Once plates have been cleared from the dinner table, resist the temptation to clean up the kitchen while guests are still present. Compulsive cleaning is definitely not compatible with good hosting. It is difficult to be attentive to guests while washing dishes and scrubbing pots and pans. However, if the mere thought of a kitchen counter overflowing with dirty dishes fills you with panic, consider containing the clutter restaurant-style in a large plastic tub until the guests are gone and you have time to clean up thoroughly.

ENJOY!

Dozens of things contribute to successful entertaining. The more planning and preparation you do, the more smoothly things will probably go. But when it comes right down to it, the most important thing of all is to help your guests enjoy themselves—and to enjoy yourself—no matter what the situation. When all is said and done, it is the shared time with family and friends that makes lasting memories.

Simple white dishes allow you to use more creative fabrics and colors for linens to create a casual feel for your table.

21

Open Face Sandwiches and
Chicken Bites

3

Appetizers, or hors d'oeuvres, may range from the simple to the elegant. They may be served as the first course in a formal meal or in place of a traditional meal. A menu of tempting hors d'oeuvres is ideal for a casual open house, a party, or a formal reception. As a buffet, appetizers should be easy to eat with one hand and should look and taste good at room temperature. You can turn any table into a beautifully arranged buffet filled with delicious foods that add flavor and style to your special occasion.

Italian Dip

Spinach Dip

Fruit Dip

Guacamole Layered Dip

Salmon Log

Spinach and Cheese Pastries

Sandwich Wraps

Cheese Bread

Open Face Sandwiches

Ham Spread

Almond-Bacon Cheese Spread

Green Chili Artichoke Spread

Parmesan Chicken Wings

Oriental Meatballs

Chicken Bites

Stuffed Mushrooms

Italian Dip

1 pound lean ground beef

½ cup onion, chopped

1 16-ounce can tomato sauce

¼ cup ketchup

1 8-ounce package cream cheese

1 cup grated Parmesan cheese

½ teaspoon garlic powder

1 teaspoon oregano

1 tablespoon dried parsley

1 4-ounce can mushrooms,
drained and chopped

⅛ teaspoon pepper

bread sticks or corn chips

Brown beef in a skillet. Add onion and cook until tender. Drain excess fat. Add tomato sauce, ketchup, cream cheese, Parmesan cheese, garlic powder, oregano, parsley, mushrooms, and pepper. Place in a microwave-safe bowl. Cover and heat for 2 minutes, then stir. Repeat until cream cheese is melted. Or heat in a saucepan over low heat, stirring constantly until cream cheese melts. Pour into a crockpot and keep warm. Serve with bread sticks or corn chips. Makes 10 to 12 servings.

Spinach Dip

1 package frozen spinach, thawed

2 cups sour cream

½ cup mayonnaise

½ cup Miracle Whip®

1 teaspoon dill weed

1 tablespoon lemon juice

½ cup finely chopped onion

¼ cup dried parsley

¼ teaspoon garlic salt

½ teaspoon horseradish

French bread, baguette, or crackers

Allow spinach to thaw and place in a colander to drain. Press excess moisture out of spinach. In a large bowl, combine spinach with sour cream, mayonnaise, Miracle Whip, dill, lemon juice, onion, parsley, garlic salt, and horseradish. Fold together until well blended. Dip is best if allowed to chill for at least one hour but may be served immediately. Serve with French bread that has been cut into cubes, slices of small baguette bread, or your favorite crackers. Makes 15 to 20 servings.

Fruit Dip

In a mixer bowl, beat together cream cheese, marshmallow creme, orange juice, and lemon juice. Beat until smooth. Refrigerate before serving. Serve with fresh fruit. Makes about 2 cups.

1 8-ounce tub strawberry or pineapple soft-style cream cheese

1 7-ounce jar marshmallow crème

1 tablespoon orange juice

1 tablespoon lemon juice

Fruit Dip with Fresh Fruit

Guacamole Layered Dip

In a medium bowl, mix refried beans, taco seasoning, and cumin. Spread this mixture in a shallow serving dish. Combine mashed avocados and 1½ cups sour cream and spread on top of the bean layer. Sprinkle onions, chilies, green pepper, and olives on top of avocado layer. In a separate bowl, combine cheeses, then sprinkle over the vegetable layer. Sprinkle diced tomatoes over cheeses.

Garnish with ½ cup sour cream by making 12 heaping mounds on top of tomatoes. Place a whole olive in each sour cream mound. Serve with corn chips or tortilla chips. Makes 15 to 20 servings.

1 large can refried beans

1 package dry taco seasoning mix

⅛ teaspoon cumin

3 avocados, peeled and mashed

1½ cups sour cream

1 bunch green onions, sliced

1 small can green chilies, diced

½ green pepper, diced

½ can black olives, sliced

¾ cup shredded longhorn or medium cheddar cheese

¾ cup shredded Monterey Jack cheese

1 tomato, diced

½ cup sour cream (for garnish)

whole olives (for garnish)

corn chips or tortilla chips

25

1 pound canned salmon

1 8-ounce package cream cheese, softened

1 tablespoon lemon juice

2 tablespoons onion, grated

½ teaspoon salt

1 teaspoon prepared horseradish

½ cup walnuts, chopped

3 tablespoons parsley, snipped fine

crackers

1 10½-ounce package frozen, chopped spinach

2 3-ounce packages cream cheese, softened

1 cup feta cheese, crumbled

½ cup grated Parmesan cheese

dash pepper

¼ cup water chestnuts, chopped very fine

1 package frozen phyllo dough sheets (18x14-inch rectangles), thawed*

⅔ cup margarine or butter, melted

Salmon Log

Drain salmon and remove the skin and bones. In a medium bowl, combine the cream cheese, lemon juice, onion, salt, and horseradish. Beat until smooth. Flake the salmon and add to the mixture; mix until well blended. Chill several hours. Combine walnuts and parsley. Shape salmon mixture into an 8x2-inch log or use a fish mold. Roll salmon log in nut mixture; chill well. Serve with crisp crackers. Makes 15 servings.

Salmon Log with Crackers

Spinach and Cheese Pastries

To make filling, allow spinach to thaw and place in a colander to drain. Press some of the excess moisture out of spinach. In a mixing bowl, stir together the cream cheese, feta cheese, Parmesan cheese, and pepper until well mixed. Stir in spinach and water chestnuts; set aside.

In a saucepan or microwave-safe bowl, melt margarine or butter and set aside. Unfold phyllo dough; cover with a damp towel or clear plastic wrap. Spread 1 sheet of phyllo dough flat. Brush with some of the melted margarine or butter. Top with another sheet of phyllo dough. Brush with more margarine or butter.

Cut the stack into two-inch strips. Place 1 rounded teaspoon of filling near the end of each strip of phyllo. Starting at the end, fold one corner of the dough diagonally over the filling, forming a triangle at the end of the strip of dough. Repeatedly fold diagonally until the entire strip of dough is folded over the filling.

Repeat with remaining dough and filling. Brush the tops of each triangle with the remaining margarine or butter. To bake, arrange pastries on an ungreased baking sheet. Bake at 375° for 20 to 25 minutes or until puffed and brown. Serve warm or cold. Makes 45 pastries.

Phyllo dough can be found in the frozen dessert section of most grocery stores.

Note: Unbaked pastries can be frozen and baked later. Transfer pastries to a freezer container or freezer bags; seal, label, and freeze. When ready to bake, arrange frozen pastries on an ungreased baking sheet. Bake at 375° for 30 minutes or until puffed and brown.

Sandwich Wraps

Place cream cheese in a small mixing bowl and beat with mixer until soft. Add the fresh rosemary and marjoram. Add garlic salt and cream; beat together until well blended. Cover and set aside.

Wash the peppers and cut them in half lengthwise; remove seeds and veins. Cut lengthwise in long, thin strips. Drop these into boiling water for approximately 1 minute so they are a little soft and pliable. Place strips in a colander and immediately run cold water over them.

Working with one tortilla at a time, spread a thin layer of cream cheese mixture on it, making sure to spread it to the edge. Sprinkle a few alfalfa sprouts on top of the cream cheese. Place 1 or 2 slices of ham on top of this. Spread a thin layer of cream cheese on the ham. (If the ham overlaps, spread the cream cheese mixture on the overlaping areas.) On the edge of the ham, place 2 pieces of the red pepper and 1 piece of the yellow pepper. Alternate the number of red and yellow peppers all the way down the ham.

Beginning at the edge, roll up the tortilla very tightly. Roll in the same direction the peppers are laid. Wrap in plastic wrap until serving time. To serve, cut slices on an angle, about ¾ to 1 inch thick. Sandwich wraps can be eaten immediately or stored, wrapped, for several days. Makes 8 wraps. Each wrap yields about 8 mini sandwiches.

* Do not use tub-style cream cheese.
** Plain or smoked turkey, or any sandwich meat, may be substituted as long as it is thinly sliced.

2 8-ounce packages cream cheese, softened*

1 teaspoon rosemary, fresh, minced fine

1 teaspoon marjoram, fresh, minced fine

¼ teaspoon garlic salt

2 tablespoons cream, half-and-half, or milk

1 red pepper

1 yellow pepper

1 package thin flour tortillas

alfalfa sprouts

8 ounces ham, thinly sliced**

Ham Sandwich Wraps

Tips and Ideas

• Basic serving trays can be used for formal or casual events. Dress them up by setting the serving table with a crisp white linen tablecloth, or dress them down by setting the table with inexpensive bamboo mats. Also consider using beds of lettuce or cabbage, fresh herbs, or rock salt to line the bottom of serving pieces.

• Replace traditional appetizer platters with cake stands or tiered serving plates.

• If the event will last for more than two hours, consider saving some of the appetizers for the second half of the party so guests can continue to sample new dishes throughout the evening.

½ cup mayonnaise

½ cup grated Parmesan cheese

1 teaspoon fresh parsley,
finely snipped

½ teaspoon Salad Supreme
salad seasoning

1 box Melba toast rounds, thinly
sliced French bread, or rolls

BREAD

white, wheat, rye, pumpernickel, or
sourdough, or a variety of these

SPREADS

Ham Spread

Almond-Bacon Cheese Spread

Green Chili Artichoke Spread

GARNISHES

small carrot curl

half a cherry tomato

thin slice of dill or sweet pickle

slice of black olive

green olive stuffed with pimento

small sprig of parsley

slice of hard boiled egg, sprinkled
with paprika

Cheese Bread

In a small bowl, combine mayonnaise and Parmesan cheese. Stir in parsley and salad seasoning. Spread 1½ to 2 teaspoons of this mixture on Melba toast rounds, French bread, or split rolls. Broil, on highest rack in oven, about 1 minute or until golden brown. Makes 15 servings Melba toast rounds or 8 servings French bread or rolls.

Open Face Sandwiches

Open face sandwiches are easy to make by using bread that is sliced lengthwise. (If you can't find this type of bread, regular sandwich bread will work.) If you are serving a large crowd you may want to use a variety of breads as well as a variety of spreads. (Recipes for ham spread, almond-bacon cheese spread, and green chili artichoke spread are found on page 29.)

Spread each slice of bread with the spread of your choice. Cut crusts off bread. (You may waste a tiny amount of sandwich spread when removing the crusts, but it is much easier to spread a whole piece of bread before you trim the crusts and cut the bread into shapes.) If you are using bread that is sliced lengthwise, cut it in one-inch slices. Cut regular sandwich bread in triangles by cutting each slice of bread diagonally in quarters. Or cut in fingers by cutting each slice of bread in thirds. You can also cut bread into shapes with small cookie cutters. (Place the cookie cutters as close together on the slice of bread as possible to minimize waste.)

Open face sandwiches can be served plain or with a garnish. Combine different spreads with different garnishes. Use your imagination to create edible garnishes in addition to those suggested.

Ham Spread

In a small mixing bowl, stir together cream cheese, mustard, and mayonnaise. Stir in ham and cheddar cheese. Cover and chill. Spread on crackers, bread, or celery sticks. Cover and store leftover spread in the refrigerator for up to 5 days. Makes enough spread for 6 slices of bread.

Variations: To make roast beef spread, substitute cooked roast beef for the ham and Swiss cheese for the cheddar cheese. To make turkey spread, substitute cooked turkey for the ham, and mozzarella cheese for the cheddar cheese.

❧

1 8-ounce tub soft-style cream cheese with chives and onion

½ teaspoon Dijon mustard

1 tablespoon mayonnaise

⅓ cup ham, fully cooked, finely chopped

¼ cup cheddar cheese, shredded

crackers, bread, or celery sticks

Almond-Bacon Cheese Spread

In a medium bowl, combine almonds, bacon, Velveeta®, green onion, and mayonnaise. Mix lightly. Spread on crackers, bread, or celery sticks. Makes enough spread for 6 slices of bread.

❧

¼ cup unblanched almonds, roasted, finely chopped

2 strips bacon, cooked crisp, crumbled

1 cup Velveeta cheese, grated

1 tablespoon green onion, chopped

½ cup mayonnaise

crackers, bread, or celery sticks

Green Chili Artichoke Spread

Place drained artichoke hearts and marinated artichoke hearts in a blender or food processor. Cover and process until finely chopped, stopping to scrape down sides as necessary.

Put blended artichokes in a medium saucepan, then stir in the cheddar cheese, cream cheese, and chili peppers. Heat over low heat, stirring constantly for 12 to 15 minutes or until the cheese is melted and the mixture is heated through. Or heat in the microwave at two-minute intervals, stirring between each interval. Serve warm with rye or pumpernickel bread, or on thin slices of toasted French bread. Makes about 2 cups.

❧

1 14-ounce can artichoke hearts, drained

1 6-ounce jar marinated artichoke hearts, drained

1 cup cheddar cheese, shredded

1 3-ounce package cream cheese

1 4-ounce can green chili peppers, drained

rye or pumpernickel party bread, or thinly sliced French bread

1 pound chicken wings

½ cup butter, melted

¼ teaspoon garlic powder

1 cup seasoned bread crumbs, dry
and finely crumbled

½ cup grated Parmesan cheese

2 tablespoons dried parsley

1 teaspoon salt

¼ teaspoon pepper

MEATBALLS

1 pound lean ground beef

2 teaspoons soy sauce

1 envelope dry onion soup mix

1 egg, beaten

⅛ teaspoon ground ginger

SAUCE

1 8-ounce can tomato sauce

1 16-ounce can whole-berry
cranberry sauce

Parmesan Chicken Wings

Preheat oven to 325°. Cut off tips from chicken wings and discard. Split remaining portion of wing at the joint to form two pieces.

In a saucepan or microwave-safe bowl, melt butter and mix in garlic powder. In a separate bowl, combine bread crumbs, Parmesan cheese, parsley, salt, and pepper. Dip the wings in the seasoned butter, then roll in crumb mixture.

Bake on a greased baking sheet (with edges) for about 50 to 55 minutes. This recipe can be prepared ahead, frozen, and baked later. Makes 6 servings.

Oriental Meatballs

In a medium bowl, combine ground beef, soy sauce, onion soup mix, egg, and ginger. Mix well. Using 1 tablespoon of mixture at a time, form into small meatballs. Brown in a skillet; discard all but 1 tablespoon of the fat.

In a medium saucepan, combine tomato sauce and cranberry sauce with the reserved tablespoon of fat. Heat through; then add the meatballs. Cover and simmer on low for about 30 minutes. Serve with toothpicks. Makes about 20 meatballs.

Tips and Ideas

• When your entire menu is composed of hors d'oeuvres, plan on two to three servings of each appetizer per guest and a minimum of eight to ten different appetizers from which to choose.

• For more than twenty guests, use both sides of a table to serve the same food or consider using several smaller serving stations rather than one big buffet. Each table could have its own color scheme, decorating theme, or type of food.

• Go for variety and visual interest in menu selection and presentation of appetizers. Garnish serving platters with fresh herbs, vegetables, fruits, and edible flowers.

Chicken Bites

In a medium bowl, beat cream cheese until smooth. Stir in chicken spread, apples, almonds, parsley, Worcestershire sauce, and garlic salt. Chill for about 30 minutes.

While mixture is chilling, preheat oven to 350°. Sprinkle wheat germ on a cookie sheet and place in the oven for 2 to 3 minutes to toast. Shape cheese mixture into small balls. Roll chicken balls in toasted wheat germ. Makes approximately 24 servings.

1 3-ounce package cream cheese, softened

1 5-ounce can chicken spread

⅓ cup apples, finely chopped

¼ cup almonds, finely chopped

2 tablespoons parsley, finely chopped

½ teaspoon Worcestershire sauce

¼ teaspoon garlic salt

½ cup wheat germ

Chicken Bites

Stuffed Mushrooms

Brown the sausage in a frying pan, stirring while cooking. (This will help it to crumble.) When sausage is done, let it drain in a colander while you prepare the rest of the filling.

Wash mushrooms and remove stems. Set the mushroom caps aside. Chop the stems to medium-fine. In a medium saucepan, combine mushroom stems, zucchini, green onion, and water. Cook and stir over medium heat until vegetables are tender. Drain. Stir sausage and Parmesan cheese into vegetable mixture.

Fill each mushroom cap with a scoop of the mixture. Place stuffed mushrooms in a 13x9x2-inch baking dish. Bake at 375° for 8 to 10 minutes or until mushroom caps are tender. Serve warm. Makes 16 to 20 servings.

½ pound mild Italian bulk sausage, browned and finely crumbled

16 to 20 large fresh mushrooms

1 small zucchini, shredded (about ¾ cup)

2 tablespoons sliced green onion

1 tablespoon water

⅓ cup grated Parmesan cheese

Lion House Quiche, Potatoes O'Brien,
and Melon Wedge with Red Grape Cluster

4

From an elegant wedding celebration to a more intimate gathering of friends, brunch is a meal with many moods and few rules. Traditionally served from late morning to early afternoon, brunch is an ideal opportunity for relaxed entertaining. Many brunch recipes may be prepared in advance so that minimal kitchen time is required for the event. When everything is done ahead of time, entertaining looks effortless and hosts can enjoy the meal with their guests.

Orange French Toast

Fruit Kabob with Fresh Fruit

Bacon Strips

Strawberry Banana Breakfast Shake

Lion House Quiche

Potatoes O'Brien

Melon Wedge with Red Grape Cluster

Crumb Cake Supreme

Orange Juice

Veggie Cheese Egg Scramble

Roasted Parmesan Potatoes

Blueberry Muffins

Peach Berry Smoothies

Orange French Toast

3 eggs

½ cup milk

½ cup orange juice

2 tablespoons sugar

1 teaspoon grated orange peel

¼ teaspoon cinnamon

⅛ teaspoon allspice

dash of salt

8 slices Texas-style bread

⅓ cup margarine or butter, melted

Grease cookie sheet. In a medium bowl, beat eggs slightly. Add milk, orange juice, sugar, orange peel, cinnamon, allspice, and salt. Beat well. Dip each slice of bread in egg mixture; place on greased cookie sheet. Cover lightly with foil, then freeze 1 to 2 hours or until completely frozen. To store, remove from freezer and stack slices of bread in freezer bag, placing wax paper between slices. Return to freezer.

To serve, heat oven to 425°. Remove desired number of slices from freezer. Brush one side of each slice with melted margarine. Place margarine-side down on ungreased cookie sheet; bake for 10 minutes. Brush top with margarine, then turn. Bake an additional 5 to 10 minutes, or until golden brown. Makes 8 slices.

Strawberry Banana Breakfast Shake

1 cup strawberries

1 medium banana, sliced

1 cup milk

½ cup plain yogurt

1 to 2 tablespoons honey

pinch of nutmeg

Wash and hull strawberries. Put strawberries, banana, milk, yogurt, honey, and nutmeg in blender. Blend until smooth. Makes 4 half-cup servings.

Tips and Ideas

• Set up a table with a blender and an attractive arrangement of fresh fruits, crushed ice, and other ingredients for smoothies. This will allow guests to create their own custom-made slushy drinks.

• To encourage conversation among guests, use round or oval tables. If your table is long, consider using the sides only and not seating guests on the ends.

• Simple, less-structured flower arrangements are most appropriate for all but the most formal brunch occasions.

Orange French Toast, Bacon Strips, and Fruit Kabob with Fresh Fruit

pastry for one 9-inch pie crust

1 teaspoon green onion, sliced

1 teaspoon green pepper,
chopped fine

¼ cup bacon, cooked and crumbled

1 cup ham, cubed small

⅓ cup bay shrimp (optional)

1 cup Swiss cheese, grated

5 eggs

1 cup half-and-half

⅛ teaspoon lemon peel

½ teaspoon salt

⅛ teaspoon dry mustard

Lion House Quiche

Fit pastry into 9-inch pie pan and sprinkle with green onions, green peppers, bacon, ham, and shrimp. Sprinkle on cheese. In a medium bowl, whip eggs with half-and-half, lemon peel, salt, and mustard. Pour over other ingredients in crust. Bake at 325° for 45 minutes. Let stand 10 minutes before serving. Makes 6 to 8 servings.

Lion House Quiche

Tips and Ideas

• Always use very fresh eggs. To tell how fresh an egg is, place it in a large bowl filled with cold water. Fresh eggs will sink to the bottom and lay horizontally. The older an egg is, the more it will tilt to an upright position. Discard any eggs that float.

• Quiche makes an excellent appetizer. To serve as a finger food, cut into 1½-inch strips on a diagonal, then cut strips into bite-size diamond-shaped pieces and arrange on a platter.

• Bake small loaves of quick breads for guests to take home. Wrapped in colored cellophane with a pretty ribbon, the loaves can be incorporated into individual place settings or placed on a tray by the door.

• Tiny glass bud vases with fresh flowers make a lovely party favor; they also double as part of the decorations until the end of the party when guests take them home.

• A large basket filled with an assortment of breads and rolls makes an inexpensive and edible centerpiece.

Potatoes O'Brien

Peel and cube potatoes. Cook in salted, boiling water for 20 minutes; drain. Spread out potatoes on buttered baking sheet. Brush tops with butter. Sprinkle with seasoned salt. Bake at 350° for 30 minutes or until browned. Remove from oven and sprinkle with red and green peppers. Makes 10 servings.

3 large potatoes

¼ cup melted butter

seasoned salt to taste

2 tablespoons red peppers, diced

2 tablespoons green peppers, diced

Crumb Cake Supreme

In a medium bowl, cream butter, shortening, and sugar. Add eggs and vanilla. In a separate bowl, combine cake flour, baking soda, and baking powder. Add sour cream and the combined dry ingredients alternately to egg mixture.

In another bowl, combine 2 tablespoons sugar, cinnamon, and chopped nuts to make the topping. Put half the batter in a well-greased and floured bundt cake pan. Sprinkle on the topping mixture. Add remaining batter. Bake at 350° for 40 to 50 minutes. Let stand in pan 10 minutes before inverting. Makes 15 servings.

This cake can also be baked in a 9x13-inch pan. Grease and flour pan, then put all the batter in pan and sprinkle with topping mixture.

* A scant 2 cups all-purpose flour may be used in place of the cake flour.

CAKE

½ cup butter

½ cup shortening

1¼ cups sugar

2 eggs

1 teaspoon vanilla

2 cups cake flour*

1 teaspoon baking soda

1 teaspoon baking powder

1 cup sour cream

TOPPING

2 tablespoons sugar

½ teaspoon cinnamon

½ cup chopped nuts

Tips and Ideas

• For a fresh, frosty garnish, use small sugared fruits and berries. Apply a thin coat of beaten egg whites to the clean, dry surface of the fruit. Sprinkle with finely granulated sugar, making sure to cover all sides. Set fruit on a cookie sheet or wire rack for several hours to dry.

• Try freezing small edible flowers or herbs in ice cube trays. Mint leaves are a perfect complement for lemonade, while violets or sprigs of lemon verbena can be added to ice water.

Veggie Cheese Egg Scramble

Cook vegetables as directed on package; drain and keep warm. In a medium bowl, combine eggs, milk, salt, basil, and pepper; beat well. Grease and heat skillet over medium-high heat. Cook onions for 1 to 2 minutes, stirring constantly. Reduce heat; add egg mixture. Stir occasionally until eggs are shiny. Add warm vegetables and sprinkle with cheese. Cover; cook 2 to 3 minutes or until cheese is melted. Makes 4 servings.

1½ cups frozen California-blend vegetables

6 eggs

2 tablespoons milk

¼ teaspoon salt

¼ teaspoon dried basil leaves

⅛ teaspoon pepper

¼ cup green onions, chopped

½ cup shredded cheddar cheese

Veggie Cheese Egg Scramble and Roasted Parmesan Potatoes

Roasted Parmesan Potatoes

Preheat oven to 450°. Line a cookie sheet with foil and spray with nonstick cooking spray. Cube potatoes and place in medium bowl; toss with oil. In another bowl, combine Parmesan cheese, parsley, paprika, garlic powder, salt, and cayenne pepper. Add to potatoes and toss to coat evenly.

Arrange potatoes on baking sheet and bake about 25 minutes or until lightly brown, turning once halfway through baking. Makes 4 servings.

4 medium potatoes, peeled

1 tablespoon oil

3 tablespoons grated Parmesan cheese

2 tablespoons fresh parsley, chopped

1 teaspoon paprika

½ teaspoon garlic powder

1 teaspoon salt

⅛ teaspoon cayenne pepper

Blueberry Muffins

Blueberry Muffins

Sift flour, sugar, baking powder, and salt into a bowl; make a well in the center. In another bowl, beat together egg, milk, and oil. Pour into well in the dry ingredients and stir until moistened. Gently fold in blueberries.

Grease muffin pans or use baking cups. Fill each cup two-thirds full of batter. Bake at 400° for 20 to 25 minutes. Makes 10 servings.

* Frozen blueberries may be substituted. Thaw and drain before using.

1¾ cups all-purpose flour

¼ cup sugar

2½ teaspoons baking powder

¾ teaspoon salt

1 egg, well-beaten

¾ cup milk

⅓ cup oil

1 cup fresh blueberries*

Peach Berry Smoothies

Combine yogurt, peaches, strawberries, and ice in blender. Cover and blend 30 to 60 seconds, or until smooth. Serve immediately. Makes 4 one-cup servings.

* Frozen strawberries may be substituted. Thaw and drain before using.

16 ounces strawberry yogurt

1 cup fresh peaches, sliced

1 cup fresh strawberries, sliced*

1 cup crushed ice

Peach Berry Smoothie

Chicken Almond Pita Sandwich, Tossed Green
Salad, Baked Chili, and Peanut Butter Cookies

5

A leisurely lunch with family and friends is one of life's great pleasures. A noontime meal can be as dressy or as casual as you like. Select a style that goes best with the occasion; a crisp white tablecloth set with gleaming silver and glassware or a red and white gingham cloth with wicker plate holders and lots of finger foods work equally well. A light but tasty entree is often the best fare for a luncheon. Experienced hosts know that a simple dish served with flair can be as impressive as the most complicated recipe.

South-of-the-Border Sandwiches

Caesar Salad

Coconut Cream Pie

Chicken Almond Pita Sandwiches

Baked Chili

Tossed Green Salad

Peanut Butter Cookies

Ranch Chicken

Lion House Dinner Rolls

Sweet and Sour Pasta Salad

Raspberry Cheesecake

South-of-the-Border Sandwiches

8 sandwich rolls, split open,
or 1 loaf French bread, sliced

½ cup olives, chopped

½ teaspoon chili powder

½ teaspoon ground cumin

¼ teaspoon salt

½ cup mayonnaise

⅓ cup sour cream

⅓ cup green onions, chopped

¾ to 1 pound cooked turkey,
thinly sliced

2 medium tomatoes, thinly sliced

2 ripe avocados, sliced

¾ cup cheddar cheese, shredded

¾ cup pepper jack or Monterey Jack
cheese, shredded

In a bowl, combine olives, chili powder, cumin, and salt; set aside 2 tablespoons of this mixture. Add the mayonnaise, sour cream, and green onions to the remaining olive mixture.

Place bread on an ungreased baking sheet and spread 1 tablespoon of the mayonnaise mixture on each slice or roll. Top with slices of turkey and tomatoes. Spread with another tablespoon of the mayonnaise mixture. Top with sliced avocados and cheeses. Sprinkle with the reserved 2 tablespoons of olive mixture.

Bake at 350° for 15 minutes or until heated through. Makes 8 to 10 servings.

South-of-the-Border Sandwiches and Caesar Salad

Caesar Salad

Wash and dry lettuce; tear into bite-size pieces. Place lettuce in large salad bowl. Combine olive oil, vinegar, Worcestershire sauce, salt, mustard, and garlic in a blender and process until smooth. Pour over lettuce and toss. Squeeze lemon juice over salad and sprinkle with pepper, Parmesan cheese, and croutons. Serve immediately. Makes 6 to 8 servings.

1 large bunch romaine lettuce

¾ cup olive oil

3 tablespoons red wine vinegar

1 teaspoon Worcestershire sauce

½ teaspoon salt

¼ teaspoon dry mustard

1 large clove garlic, minced

juice of ½ fresh lemon

dash pepper

½ cup Parmesan cheese, shredded

seasoned croutons

Coconut Cream Pie

Mix cornstarch, sugar, and salt in a 3-quart saucepan. Add milk and half-and-half; cook over medium heat until smooth and thick, stirring constantly.

Place egg yolks in a bowl. Pour a small amount of the hot mixture into the egg yolks; blend thoroughly, then pour back into saucepan. Cook another 2 or 3 minutes.

Remove from heat and add butter and vanilla. Stir in ½ cup of the coconut. Pour into baked pie crust. Chill 3 to 4 hours.

When ready to serve, whip and sweeten the cream, then spread over pie. Top with the remaining ½ cup of coconut. Makes 8 servings.

1 baked 9-inch pie crust

5 tablespoons cornstarch

1 cup sugar

¼ teaspoon salt

2½ cups milk

¾ cup half-and-half

3 egg yolks

2 teaspoons butter or margarine

1 teaspoon vanilla

1 cup coconut (toasted, if desired)

1 cup whipping cream

1 8-ounce package cream cheese, softened

½ cup mayonnaise

3 tablespoons milk

1 teaspoon lemon juice

3 cups chicken, cooked and diced

⅓ cup red pepper, chopped

⅓ cup green pepper, chopped

3 tablespoons green onion, chopped

1 teaspoon dry mustard

½ teaspoon salt

¼ teaspoon pepper

⅓ cup slivered almonds

3 large pieces pita bread, halved

alfalfa sprouts (optional)

Chicken Almond Pita Sandwiches

In a mixing bowl, beat cream cheese, mayonnaise, milk, and lemon juice until smooth. Stir in cooked chicken, red and green peppers, green onion, mustard, salt, and pepper. Refrigerate.

Just before serving, stir in almonds. Spoon about ½ to ¾ cup filling into each pita half. Top with sprouts, if desired. Makes 3 to 6 servings.

Chicken Almond Pita Sandwich and Tossed Green Salad

Tips and Ideas

• Pack a picnic. Remember that you don't have to cook food outdoors to enjoy eating it outdoors. If properly packaged, most dishes can be transported with minimal fuss.

• When eating out-of-doors, plan for Mother Nature as you pack your linens. Tape quarters to the backside edges of your tablecloth to weigh it down, and use a napkin holder to prevent the napkins from blowing away.

• Create an outdoor garden dining room with flowering plants in pots, decorative birdhouses or bird cages, and a tabletop water fountain. For background music, play a relaxing recording of nature sounds, such as bird calls, waterfalls, or sounds from a tropical rain forest.

Baked Chili

In a Dutch oven or large 4-quart pan, cook beef, onion, and green pepper over medium heat until meat is cooked through. Drain. Rinse and drain kidney beans; add to meat mixture. Add drained corn, tomato sauce, tomatoes, green chilies, chili powder, sugar, salt, cumin, and garlic powder. Bring to a boil, stirring occasionally. Reduce heat; cover and simmer for 10 minutes.

Meanwhile, combine flour, cornmeal, baking powder, and salt in a medium bowl. In a separate bowl, beat egg, milk, and sour cream until smooth; stir into dry ingredients just until moistened. Set aside.

Transfer chili to an ungreased 9x13-inch baking dish. Drop biscuit batter by heaping teaspoonfuls onto hot chili. Bake uncovered at 400° for 15 to 17 minutes or until biscuits are lightly browned. Makes 8 servings.

CHILI

1 pound ground beef

1 large onion, chopped

1 large green pepper, chopped

1 16-ounce can kidney beans, rinsed and drained

1 15 ¼-ounce can whole kernel corn, drained

1 15-ounce can tomato sauce

1 14 ½-ounce can diced tomatoes

1 4-ounce can diced green chilies

2 teaspoons chili powder

½ teaspoon sugar

1 teaspoon salt

1 teaspoon ground cumin

½ teaspoon garlic powder

CORN BREAD BISCUITS

1 cup all-purpose flour

1 cup cornmeal

2 teaspoons baking powder

⅛ teaspoon salt

1 egg

½ cup milk

½ cup sour cream

Tips and Ideas

• Fill a wooden box with small herb plants, such as oregano, chives, and lemon verbena, and use as a centerpiece. Give the plants to guests as they depart.

• A basket or platter of colorful red, green, yellow, and orange bell peppers makes an inexpensive and appealing summer centerpiece.

• A roll of bold-striped awning fabric makes a great stain-resistant table cover that can be used year after year for outdoor entertaining.

DRESSING

2 tablespoons mayonnaise

1 tablespoon chopped parsley

dash of garlic salt

3 tablespoons lemon juice

2 tablespoons vinegar

salt and pepper to taste

1 teaspoon paprika

½ cup heavy cream

SALAD

1 large head crisped lettuce

7 green onions, chopped
(use part of green tops)

¼ head red cabbage, chopped

¼ large head white cabbage,
chopped

3 to 4 medium tomatoes,
cut in wedges

e

5¼ cups all-purpose flour

2 teaspoons baking soda

1 teaspoon salt

1 cup butter

¾ cup shortening

1¾ cups sugar

1¾ cups brown sugar

4 eggs

1 teaspoon vanilla

¾ cup peanut butter

Tossed Green Salad

In a medium bowl or salad dressing container, combine mayonnaise, parsley, garlic salt, lemon juice, vinegar, salt, pepper, paprika, and cream. Let dressing ingredients stand for at least 30 minutes.

Wash and drain lettuce and cabbages. Tear lettuce into bite-size pieces in a large bowl. Add onions and red and white cabbage; toss. Pour dressing over greens. Do not mix, but toss lightly just before serving. Garnish with tomato wedges. Makes about 12 servings.

Peanut Butter Cookies

Preheat oven to 350°. Line a cookie sheet with wax paper and set aside.

Mix flour, baking soda, and salt together in a medium bowl and set aside. In a large mixing bowl, cream together butter, shortening, sugar, brown sugar, eggs, and vanilla. Stir in peanut butter. Add flour mixture a little at a time and stir until well blended.

Drop dough by tablespoonfuls onto cookie sheet. Using a fork dipped in flour, flatten each cookie slightly in a crisscross pattern. Bake for 8 to 10 minutes or until slightly golden around the edges. Do not overbake. Makes 5 dozen 3-inch cookies.

Ranch Chicken

In a shallow bowl, combine the cornflakes, Parmesan cheese, and salad dressing mix. Dip chicken in melted butter, then roll in cornflake mixture to coat.

Place chicken breasts in a greased 9x13-inch baking dish. Bake, uncovered, at 350° for 45 minutes or until chicken juices run clear. Makes 8 servings.

¾ cup cornflakes, crushed

¾ cup grated Parmesan cheese

1 package ranch salad dressing mix

8 boneless, skinless chicken breast halves

½ cup butter or margarine, melted

Lion House Dinner Rolls

See recipe on page 57.

Lion House Dinner Rolls

Tips and Ideas

• Allow one set of salt and pepper shakers for every six people. Small bowls of coarse salt and pepper in decorative dishes or shells are a good alternative.

• Always have plenty of cool drinks available, and be sure to have more than enough ice on hand.

SALAD

1 16-ounce package tricolor
spiral pasta

1 medium red onion, chopped

1 medium tomato, chopped

1 medium cucumber, peeled,
seeded, and chopped

1 medium green pepper, chopped

2 tablespoons fresh parsley, minced

DRESSING

1½ cups sugar

½ cup vinegar

1 tablespoon ground mustard

1 teaspoon garlic powder

1 teaspoon salt (optional)

1 package white cake mix

2 8-ounce packages cream cheese,
softened at room temperature

4 cups powdered sugar

1 pint whipping cream, whipped

2 16-ounce cans raspberry
pie filling

Sweet and Sour Pasta Salad

Cook pasta according to package directions; drain and rinse with cold water. Place in a large serving bowl. Add the onion, tomato, cucumber, green pepper, and parsley; set aside.

In a saucepan, combine the sugar, vinegar, mustard, garlic powder, and salt. Cook over medium-low heat for 10 minutes or until sugar is dissolved. Pour over pasta salad and toss to coat. Cover and refrigerate for 2 hours. Makes 16 servings.

Raspberry Cheesecake

Preheat oven to 350°. Grease and flour two 9x13-inch baking pans. Prepare cake according to package directions. Pour half of cake batter in each pan. Bake for 20 minutes or until cakes test done. Remove from oven and cool.

In a medium bowl, whip cream cheese and powdered sugar together until fluffy. Whip whipping cream separately, then add to cream cheese mixture. Divide the mixture and spread half of it onto each cake. Then spread one can pie filling on top of each cream cheese layer. Refrigerate until ready to serve. Makes 24 to 30 servings.

Ranch Chicken, Lion House Dinner Roll, and Sweet and Sour Pasta Salad

Pineapple Chicken Salad

Food always tastes better when shared with family and friends. A spur-of-the-moment gathering, a light dinner for your club meeting, or an informal backyard party call for a simple approach with a menu that can be easily prepared and served. A casual meal can be dressed up by adding a cheese and fruit tray or vegetables and dip; look for seasonal fruits and vegetables as fresh and easy additions to any menu.

Spinach Salad with Strawberries

Oatmeal Rolls

Homemade Peppermint Ice Cream

Pineapple Ham Salad

Corn Bread

Bananas Foster over Ice Cream

Grilled Chicken Teriyaki and Rice

Lion House Dinner Rolls

Peach Cobbler

DRESSING

2 tablespoons red wine vinegar

3 tablespoons sugar

½ cup oil

½ teaspoon dry mustard

½ teaspoon salt

½ cup strawberry jam

SALAD

⅓ cup sugar

1 cup cashew pieces

15 wontons, cut into thin strips

1 large head red leaf lettuce, washed and broken into pieces

1 package fresh spinach, with stems trimmed

⅓ cup bacon pieces, cooked and well drained

½ cup red bell pepper, chopped

1 purple onion, sliced

1 cup strawberries, sliced

⁓

2 cups quick-cooking oatmeal

2 cups boiling water

1 cup butter

1½ tablespoons yeast

2 large eggs

2 teaspoons salt

⅜ cup sugar

4½ cups all-purpose flour

2 tablespoons butter, melted

Spinach Salad with Strawberries

To make dressing, mix together vinegar, sugar, oil, mustard, salt, and strawberry jam. Mix until all ingredients are well blended. Set aside.

Heat a medium frying pan and add sugar and nuts. Stir constantly over medium heat until nuts are coated and slightly browned. Remove from heat and set aside.

Fry wontons in hot cooking oil and drain onto paper towels.

When ready to serve salad, put lettuce, spinach, bacon, red pepper, onion, and strawberries into a large bowl and toss. Add salad dressing and toss. Add sugared nuts and wontons last. Makes 10 servings.

Variation: Use fresh raspberries and raspberry jam instead of strawberries and strawberry jam. Substitute almonds for cashews. When fresh berries aren't available, substitute dried cranberries.

Oatmeal Rolls

In a large bowl, measure oatmeal and pour the boiling water over the top of it. Stir slightly so all of the oatmeal is moistened. Cut the butter into small chunks and place on top of oatmeal mixture; set aside until butter is melted and the mixture has cooled.

Sprinkle yeast on top of oatmeal mixture. Add eggs, salt, sugar, and flour. Mix on low speed for 8 to 10 minutes. The dough will be very soft and sticky, but do not add more flour.

Allow dough to rise until it doubles in size. Roll out on a well-floured board until dough is about ¼-inch thick. Brush with melted butter and cut with 3½-inch round cutter. Fold each round in half, then take two rounds and fold them so the ends interlock; round edges up, folded sides down.

Place rolls in regular-size muffin tins that have been sprayed with nonstick spray. Let rise until double in size. Bake at 375° for 10 to 12 minutes. Rolls should be light golden brown. If they are dark golden brown, they are overdone and will be dry. Makes 2 dozen rolls.

Spinach Salad with Strawberries

4 eggs

2½ cups sugar

5 cups milk

4 cups heavy whipping cream

4 teaspoons vanilla

½ teaspoon salt

1½ cups crushed peppermint
candies

SALAD

1 medium pineapple

2 cups cooked ham, diced

2 medium stalks celery, sliced

1 cup red seedless grapes

½ cup cashews

lettuce leaves

DRESSING

¾ cup mayonnaise

2 teaspoons lemon juice

½ teaspoon ground ginger

⅛ teaspoon garlic salt

Homemade Peppermint Ice Cream

In a large bowl, beat eggs; add sugar gradually. Beat until mixture is stiff. Add milk, whipping cream, vanilla, salt, and crushed candy. Mix thoroughly. Pour into cold canister and freeze (4- to 5-quart freezer recommended). Makes 12 servings.

Pineapple Ham Salad

Remove top from pineapple then cut pineapple crosswise into 5 slices. Cut pineapple from each slice, leaving ½-inch ring. Reserve rings; core and cut up remaining pineapple. In a large bowl, toss pineapple chunks, ham, celery, and grapes. In a separate bowl, mix mayonnaise, lemon juice, ginger, and garlic salt to make dressing. Toss into ham mixture. Just before serving, fold in cashews. Arrange pineapple rings on lettuce leaves. Fill with salad and garnish with a small cluster of grapes. Makes 5 servings.

Variation: Two cups cooked, diced chicken breasts may be used instead of ham to make pineapple chicken salad.

Pineapple Chicken Salad

Tips and Ideas

• A vintage enamelware colander makes a generous and unbreakable bowl for fresh fruit.

Corn Bread

In a medium bowl, blend together flour, sugar, baking powder, salt, and corn meal. Stir in eggs and milk until smooth; add melted margarine, just until blended. Do not overmix.

Pour into a well-greased loaf pan. Bake at 425° for 30 to 40 minutes. Cool for 10 minutes, then turn out of pan. Serve warm or cold. Makes 5 servings.

1⅔ cups all-purpose flour

⅔ cup sugar

5 teaspoons baking powder

1 teaspoon salt

1⅔ cups yellow corn meal

2 eggs, beaten

1⅔ cups milk

⅓ cup margarine, melted

Bananas Foster over Ice Cream

Put margarine, brown sugar, and corn syrup in a microwave-safe bowl; microwave for 1 minute on full power. Stir for 1 minute, then add extract and bananas. Microwave for 30 seconds. Serve over vanilla ice cream. Makes 5 servings.

¼ cup margarine

¼ cup brown sugar, firmly packed

2 tablespoons light corn syrup

½ teaspoon pineapple extract

2 bananas, sliced

vanilla ice cream

Tips and Ideas

- Try serving ice cream in small flower pots lined with foil muffin cups and topped with edible flowers such as violets or pansies.

- Casual events call for less formal decorations. Oversized baskets and bowls, wooden crates, galvanized buckets, and weathered pots make charming containers for fruits, vegetables, and flowers.

- A row of potted plants down the center of the table makes an easy centerpiece. Or put a small potted plant at each place setting for your guests to take home.

- For a homespun centerpiece, fill a big basket with homemade jams or jellies. Cover each jar with a piece of fabric to match your color scheme and tie with a piece of jute twine. Give each guest a jar of your preserves as a party favor.

- If you plan to entertain out-of-doors, go to the location a few days ahead at the same time of day you will be serving your guests on the actual day of the party. This will help you assess how much sun or shade to plan for.

- For extra protection from insects at outdoor parties, light up the night with citronella candles. The sharp lemon scent is effective in repelling bugs and flying insects. (Several small candles are more effective than one large candle.)

Grilled Chicken Teriyaki and Rice

1 large can pineapple chunks

½ cup soy sauce

1 tablespoon molasses

2 tablespoons brown sugar

¼ cup oil

3 tablespoons cider vinegar

1 teaspoon garlic powder

6 chicken breasts, boned and skinned

1 green bell pepper, cut into julienne strips

rice

Drain pineapple chunks and reserve liquid. Combine pineapple juice with soy sauce, molasses, brown sugar, oil, vinegar, and garlic powder. Marinate chicken breasts in the refrigerator in this mixture for at least 6 to 8 hours.

Drain liquid; grill chicken on barbecue. Slice into strips; add pineapple chunks and green peppers. Serve over cooked rice. Makes 6 servings.

Grilled Chicken Teriyaki and Rice

Tips and Ideas

• For evening outdoor entertaining, carefully consider the lighting you will need. Candles protected by glass or tin are a good option for tabletops. They also look terrific suspended from tree limbs. Torches, votives, or luminaries can light walkways or patios. Remember, never leave candles unattended.

• Salad greens can be prepared at least an hour ahead. Wash the greens thoroughly (spinach leaves are notoriously gritty), discarding any limp or coarse outer leaves. Shake the leaves to remove as much water as possible, then lay them on long pieces of paper towel and roll up the towel so it absorbs any remaining excess moisture. Put the wrapped leaves in a plastic bag and leave them in the refrigerator crisper drawer until you are ready to make the salad.

• To add to the romance of an evening get-together, string tiny white lights on tree branches, deck railings, fences, or the underside of a patio umbrella. Lights are a nice touch whether or not you will be dining out-of-doors.

Lion House Dinner Rolls

In a large bowl, mix yeast and water and let stand 5 minutes. Add sugar, shortening, salt, dry milk, egg, and 2 cups of the flour. Beat together until smooth. Gradually add remaining flour until soft dough is formed.

Turn onto a lightly floured surface and knead until smooth and elastic. Place in a greased bowl; cover and let rise until dough doubles in bulk. Punch down; divide into thirds.

Roll out one third of dough into a circle; cut into 12 pie-shaped pieces. Starting at the wide end, roll up each piece into a crescent. Place on greased baking sheet with point on bottom. Repeat with remainder of dough.

Brush tops with melted butter or margarine. Let rise until double in size. Bake at 400° for 15 minutes. Serve warm with honey butter or cran-raspberry butter, if desired. Makes 3 dozen rolls.

To make honey butter, whip butter; add vanilla and egg yolk. Gradually whip in honey until light and fluffy. Makes 1½ cups.

To make cran-raspberry butter, combine all ingredients in a mixing bowl; beat on high for 5 minutes. Mixture should be creamy. Spoon into a dish; cover and refrigerate for 24 hours. Makes 3½ cups.

See photograph on page 47.

Peach Cobbler

In a medium bowl, cream together margarine and sugar. Add flour, baking powder, salt, and milk. Mix well and spread into a well-greased 9x9-inch pan.

Drain peaches, reserving ¾ cup liquid. Slice peaches and place on top of batter. Sprinkle with cinnamon and sugar; pour reserved liquid over top. Bake at 375° for 45 minutes. Serve warm or cold with whipped cream or vanilla ice cream. Makes 8 to 10 servings.

* Canned sliced peaches may be substituted.

ROLLS

2 tablespoons yeast

2 cups warm water

⅓ cup sugar

⅓ cup shortening, margarine, or butter

2 teaspoons salt

⅔ cup nonfat dry milk

I egg

5 to 6 cups all-purpose flour

butter or margarine, melted

HONEY BUTTER

½ cup softened butter

¼ teaspoon vanilla

I egg yolk

I cup honey

CRAN-RASPBERRY BUTTER

I cup canned whole-berry cranberry sauce

½ cup raspberry preserves

2 cups butter, softened

I tablespoon powdered sugar

¼ cup margarine

½ cup sugar

I cup all-purpose flour

2 teaspoons baking powder

¼ teaspoon salt

½ cup milk

I quart bottled peaches, drained and sliced*

cinnamon and sugar

whipped cream or vanilla ice cream

Glazed Broccoli with Almonds, Refrigerator Rolls,
Baked Salmon, Fruit and Lettuce Salad, and Rice Pilaf

7

A dinner buffet with an array of delicious foods is ideal for almost any occasion. Both a visual and edible feast, a buffet is more adaptable than a sit-down dinner, allows for a larger guest list, and gives the hosts more freedom to move between guests to entertain. The word *buffet* means sideboard in French, and a sideboard table was traditionally used for serving food, but a long or round table works equally well. Typical dinner buffets include one or two entrees, vegetable dishes, a rice or potato selection, salads, a roll or bread, and one or more desserts. Let the occasion determine the menu, and remember that dishes which can be completely or partially prepared ahead will leave more time for hosts to join family and friends.

Dinner Buffet

Oven Kalua Pork

Baked Salmon

Rice Pilaf

Glazed Broccoli with Almonds

Nutmeg Spinach Soufflé

Fruit and Lettuce Salad

Tomato and Cucumber Salad

Refrigerator Rolls

Chocolate Cream Cake

❧

Chicken Dijon

Buffet Ham

Potato Casserole

Green Beans Parmesan

Crookneck Squash Scallop

Poppy Seed Spinach Salad

Apple Salad

Hot Orange Rolls

Chiffon Cake

❧

Chicken Cordon Bleu

Swedish Meatballs

Rice with Mushrooms

Marinated Tomato Slices

Vegetable Medley

Sarah's Salad

Coleslaw Cardinal

Lion House Dinner Rolls

Pecan Bars

Cream Cheese Brownies

Lemon Bars

Oven Kalua Pork

¼ cup soy sauce

3 tablespoons coarse salt

1 teaspoon Worcestershire sauce

1 small piece fresh ginger root, crushed*

1 clove garlic, crushed

5 to 6 pounds boneless pork roast

1 teaspoon liquid wood smoke flavoring

In a small bowl, combine soy sauce, salt, Worcestershire sauce, ginger, and garlic. Mix well. Lay 3 sheets of aluminum foil out, one on top of another. Place roast in center of aluminum foil; rub with soy sauce mixture and sprinkle liquid smoke on top. Fold all 3 sheets of aluminum foil over top of roast and secure tightly. Place wrapped meat in a baking pan. Roast at 375° for 5 hours. Shred the pork before serving. Makes 8 servings.

* 1 teaspoon ground ginger may be substituted for ginger root.

Baked Salmon

1 small, whole salmon (about 4 pounds)

1 teaspoon instant minced onion

1 teaspoon minced dill pickle

½ teaspoon dried parsley flakes

1 cup bread crumbs

¼ cup evaporated milk

2 tablespoons butter

1 teaspoon salt

⅛ teaspoon pepper

½ cup water

1 lemon, cut in wedges

Preheat oven to 350°. Clean the fish; pat dry with paper towels. In a medium bowl, combine the onion, pickle, parsley, and bread crumbs. Add the milk and let soak. Place the fish in a greased baking dish and stuff with the crumb mixture. Dot the surface with butter and sprinkle with salt and pepper. Add the water to the dish and place in preheated oven. Bake, uncovered, about 1 hour, basting the fish frequently with the liquid from the bottom of the dish. (Fish may be baked in a baking bag, if desired.) Serve hot with wedges of fresh lemon. Makes 6 servings.

Baked Salmon Garnished with Lemon and Cucumber Slices

Rice Pilaf

Melt butter in hot frying pan. Add rice, onion, and celery; stir and cook until slightly brown. Add chicken broth. Cover and simmer on low heat until moisture has been absorbed and rice is tender. Add parsley and almonds just before serving. Toss lightly. Makes 8 one-half cup servings.

2 tablespoons butter or margarine

1 cup uncooked rice

¼ cup onion, minced

⅓ cup celery, minced

3 cups hot chicken broth

2 tablespoons parsley, chopped

¼ cup slivered almonds

Glazed Broccoli with Almonds

Preheat oven to 375°. Grease a 9x9-inch baking pan. Separate broccoli; trim stems, and wash thoroughly. Add salt and broccoli to boiling water and cook for 12 minutes or until barely tender. Drain and arrange in baking pan.

While broccoli is cooking, prepare sauce. Dissolve bouillon cube in ¾ cup hot water. In a saucepan, melt butter or margarine; blend in flour. Gradually stir cream and dissolved bouillon cube into flour mixture; cook over medium heat, stirring constantly, until thickened and smooth. Remove from heat and stir in lemon juice and salt and pepper to taste. Pour sauce over broccoli. Sprinkle with Parmesan cheese and almonds. Bake for 20 minutes or until golden brown. Makes 6 to 8 servings.

Two 10-ounce packages frozen broccoli may be substituted.

2 pounds fresh broccoli*

½ teaspoon salt

1 chicken bouillon cube

¾ cup hot water

¼ cup butter or margarine

¼ cup all-purpose flour

1 cup light cream

2 tablespoons lemon juice

salt and pepper

¼ cup grated Parmesan cheese

¼ cup slivered blanched almonds

Tips and Ideas

- Surround a platter of fish with lemon wedges and parsley, or tuck bouquets of herbs such as rosemary, sage, basil, or chives around the food.

- Many vegetables can be used as containers for dip. Create "natural" bowls of various sizes from hollowed out peppers, squash, zucchini, or pie pumpkins. Thoroughly rinse and drain vegetables before filling with dip.

Nutmeg Spinach Soufflé

1 pound fresh spinach

2 tablespoons margarine

2 tablespoons all-purpose flour

1 teaspoon salt

1 cup milk

4 egg yolks, beaten

¼ cup onion, chopped

⅛ teaspoon nutmeg

4 egg whites

¼ teaspoon cream of tartar

3 tablespoons grated Parmesan cheese

Wash spinach; cook in small amount of salted water. Drain and press out all excess water; chop spinach. Melt margarine in saucepan; add flour and salt and blend. Gradually add milk and stir until thickened. Gradually add beaten egg yolks. Stir in spinach, onion, and nutmeg. Beat egg whites and cream of tartar until stiff. Fold into spinach mixture. Pour into greased soufflé dish. Sprinkle with Parmesan cheese. Bake at 375° for 50 minutes or until set. Makes 6 servings.

Fruit and Lettuce Salad

SALAD

2 medium apples, cut into chunks

2 medium oranges, peeled and sectioned

lettuce leaves

4 cups shredded lettuce

½ cup celery, chopped

2 bananas, sliced

1 cup pecans, broken into pieces

1 cup cherry tomatoes, halved

DRESSING

⅓ cup mayonnaise

¼ cup whipping cream

2 tablespoons prepared mustard

¼ teaspoon celery seed

In a medium bowl, toss together the apples and oranges. Cover and chill. Line a large serving bowl with lettuce leaves. Combine the shredded lettuce and celery and place in lettuce-lined bowl. Cover and chill.

When ready to serve, toss apples and oranges with sliced bananas. Arrange fruit over the shredded lettuce in the serving bowl. Sprinkle with pecans. Arrange cherry tomato halves around the edge and on top of the salad.

To make dressing, whisk together mayonnaise, cream, mustard, and celery seed in a small bowl. Pour over fruit mixture. Before serving, toss gently to coat all ingredients. Makes 10 servings.

Tomato and Cucumber Salad

Slice tomatoes and cucumbers in ⅛-inch slices. In a medium serving bowl, combine tomatoes, cucumbers, onion, and garbanzo beans. In a separate bowl, whisk together vinegar, oil, sugar, salt, and oregano or parsley. Add pepper to taste. Pour dressing over vegetables and toss to mix well. Let stand in refrigerator for 1 hour before serving. Makes 10 servings.

3 medium tomatoes, sliced

2 medium cucumbers, peeled and sliced

½ small onion, chopped

1 16-ounce can garbanzo beans

¼ cup red wine vinegar

¼ cup vegetable oil

2 teaspoons sugar

½ teaspoon salt

½ teaspoon oregano or ½ teaspoon dried parsley flakes

pepper to taste

Refrigerator Rolls

In a small saucepan, scald the milk. Add butter and ¼ cup sugar to hot milk. Cool. Combine yeast, 1 tablespoon sugar, and lukewarm water. Let stand 5 minutes to soften yeast.

Add salt to flour; set aside. In a large bowl, combine milk and yeast mixtures, and add 1 cup of the flour. Add eggs and beat well. Continue adding flour gradually, beating until smooth after each addition. (This is a soft dough, and most or all of the flour can be handled by an electric mixer.)

Cover bowl and place out of draft. Let dough rise until it triples in size. Punch down. Cover again and place in refrigerator overnight, or until thoroughly chilled. (Dough will keep well up to 3 days.) When ready for use, remove from refrigerator and roll and shape while cold. (You can handle a much softer dough if it is chilled.) Place on greased pans. Brush dough with melted butter. Let rolls rise 1 to 1½ hours. Bake rolls at 375° for 10 to 15 minutes or until done. Makes 2½ dozen rolls.

Note: This dough can be left to rise for 5 to 6 hours without doing it any harm. It's a good recipe to use for church dinners or parties when you don't know how long rolls will have to stand before you can bake them.

1 cup milk

¼ cup butter or margarine

¼ cup sugar

1 tablespoon yeast

1 tablespoon sugar

¼ cup lukewarm water

2 teaspoons salt

4 cups all-purpose flour

3 eggs

2 tablespoons butter, melted

CAKE

1 package devil's food cake mix

CHOCOLATE FROSTING

4 tablespoons cocoa

3 cups powdered sugar

4 tablespoons butter or margarine, softened

2 to 3 tablespoons milk

1 teaspoon vanilla

STABILIZED WHIPPING CREAM

1 tablespoon unflavored gelatin

¼ cup cold water

3 cups heavy whipping cream

¾ cup powdered sugar

1½ teaspoons vanilla

Chocolate Cream Cake

Prepare and bake cake mix according to package directions, baking in two 9-inch round layers. Cool, then split both layers horizontally. You will only use three of the four rounds of cake. (The fourth layer may be frozen for the next time you make the cake.) While cake is baking, prepare chocolate frosting and stabilized whipping cream.

To make frosting, mix cocoa and powdered sugar in mixing bowl. Add softened butter, milk, and vanilla. Beat until smooth.

To make stabilized whipping cream, combine gelatin with water in a small saucepan. Let stand until thick. Over low heat, stir constantly until gelatin is just dissolved. Remove from heat and allow to cool slightly. (Mixture should still be liquid.) In a large mixing bowl, whip the cream, powdered sugar, and vanilla until slightly thick. Turn mixer on low and gradually add the gelatin, then beat on high until the cream is thick. (Stabilized whipping cream will hold up for 4 to 5 days without separating. It can be used in any recipe that calls for whipped cream or nondairy whipped topping.)

To assemble the cake, place one layer of cake on a serving plate. Put half of the stabilized whipping cream on top of the layer of cake. Spread evenly, being careful to leave about a ½-inch border around the edge of the cake with no cream. Then put another layer of cake on top of the cream. Repeat the above steps for a total of five layers: chocolate cake layer, cream layer, chocolate cake layer, cream layer, and chocolate cake layer. Gently push down on the cake to set the layers together. Frost entire cake with chocolate frosting.

Tips and Ideas

• Ice rings thaw much more slowly than ice cubes and will keep punch from becoming diluted as quickly. Freeze some of the punch in a ring mold or bundt pan. To release the frozen ring from the mold, set it in a pan of hot water just long enough to loosen the ring. Then invert the ring into a punch bowl so that the rounded side is facing up. For a fancier ring, pour an inch of liquid into the mold and freeze. Then place washed berries around the ring, add liquid to cover, and freeze.

• Place desserts on a separate table or in another room where they can be set out after the main meal has been served.

Chicken Dijon

Skin and debone chicken. Place in a large saucepan and add the ¾ cup water, grape juice, onion, lemon juice, bouillon cube, peppercorns, and thyme. Cover and simmer 15 minutes or until done. Remove chicken and keep warm in a serving dish.

Strain chicken stock and return to pan; add honey, mustard, and mushrooms. Bring to a boil and simmer 10 minutes. Make a paste of flour and 2 tablespoons water and stir into stock. Stir until slightly thickened. Spoon over chicken. Garnish with sprigs of thyme and lemon slices, if desired. Makes 4 servings.

4 chicken breast halves

¾ cup water

¾ cup white grape juice

1 small onion, sliced

3 tablespoons lemon juice

1 chicken bouillon cube

12 whole peppercorns

1 teaspoon thyme

1 tablespoon honey

2 teaspoons Dijon mustard

1½ cups fresh mushrooms, sliced

2 teaspoons all-purpose flour

2 tablespoons water

sprigs of fresh thyme (for garnish)

lemon slices (for garnish)

Buffet Ham

Have butcher cut ham in half-inch slices. Spread one side of each ham slice generously with mustard. Arrange in large roasting pan, slices overlapping. In a medium bowl, combine orange juice, syrup, allspice, mace, cinnamon, and paprika; pour over ham. Bake uncovered for 30 minutes at 350°.

Remove from oven and pour on the combined creams. Return to oven and bake about 1 hour longer. Spoon hot sauce over each slice as it is served. Makes about 16 servings.

1 boneless ham (7 or 8 pounds)

prepared mustard

1½ cups orange juice

1½ cups maple syrup

1 teaspoon allspice

½ teaspoon mace

½ teaspoon cinnamon

2 teaspoons paprika

3 cups cream (part whipping cream, part half-and-half)

Chicken Dijon, Hot Orange Rolls, and Potato Casserole

Potato Casserole

Boil whole, unpared potatoes until tender; drain and peel. Shred coarsely and place in a 2- or 3-quart casserole dish. Pour melted butter over potatoes. In a bowl, mix together soup, sour cream, milk, green onions, and cheese. Pour evenly over potatoes. Do not mix.

Mix corn flake crumbs or bread crumbs with melted butter and Parmesan cheese. Cover the top of potatoes with this mixture. Bake 30 minutes at 325°. Makes 8 to 10 servings.

CASSEROLE

5 large potatoes, unpeeled

3 tablespoons butter or margarine, melted

1 10½-ounce can cream of chicken soup

1 cup sour cream

1 cup milk

3 tablespoons green onions, finely chopped

¾ cup sharp cheddar cheese, shredded

TOPPING

¾ cup corn flake crumbs or dry bread crumbs

2 tablespoons butter or margarine, melted

3 tablespoons grated Parmesan cheese

Tips and Ideas

- Unless individual table settings have been provided, guests should be able to use a fork or spoon to eat any food served. It is difficult to use a knife while balancing a plate on your lap.

- Paper napkins are perfectly acceptable for buffet-style entertaining. Provide a sufficient quantity so that each guest may have more than one if they like.

- Precut butter into individual serving-size pieces and allow more than one pat of butter per guest.

- For a fancy fruit bowl, cut a watermelon in half lengthwise. Hollow out fruit. Cut the edge of the "bowl" in an up-and-down pattern like a crown. Cut removed watermelon into bite-size pieces and add chunks of cantaloupe, honeydew, pineapple, strawberries, and other desired fruits. Serve fruit in the melon bowl.

- To make carrot curl garnishes, cut trimmed and peeled carrots into thin strips (about ⅛ of an inch thick) and refrigerate overnight in a bowl of ice water. Strips will begin to curl after two or three hours.

Green Beans Parmesan

6 ounces bacon, diced

¾ cup onion, finely chopped

6 cups canned cut green beans

¼ teaspoon salt*

½ cup corn flake crumbs

½ cup grated Parmesan cheese

Fry bacon until crisp; remove from fat and drain. Cook onions in bacon fat until tender, stirring constantly. Drain off most of bacon fat. In a saucepan, heat green beans; drain well. Add bacon, onion, salt, corn flake crumbs, and Parmesan cheese to green beans; toss lightly until thoroughly mixed. Serve immediately. Makes 12 one-half cup servings.

Add more or less salt depending on the saltiness of the beans.

Crookneck Squash Scallop

3 medium-size yellow crookneck squash

1 cup water

½ teaspoon salt

1 medium onion, sliced

¼ cup margarine

¼ cup all-purpose flour

2½ cups milk

1 teaspoon salt

2 tablespoons chopped pimiento

1 cup cracker crumbs

3 tablespoons melted margarine

Wash and slice squash. Bring water and salt to a boil; cook squash in salted water for 8 to 10 minutes. Add onion and continue cooking for another 5 minutes. Drain vegetables; put into casserole dish.

Make white sauce by melting ¼ cup margarine and adding flour; stir to make roux. Slowly add milk and stir over medium heat until thickened. Stir in salt and pimiento. Pour sauce over squash.

In a small bowl, mix cracker crumbs and 3 tablespoons melted margarine. Sprinkle on top of casserole. Bake at 350° for 20 minutes. Makes 6 servings.

Tips and Ideas

- When planning the centerpiece, remember that the food will be on display with the china and tablecloth. Often, the food itself can serve as the centerpiece.

- Use hot plates, chafing dishes, or warming trays to keep the food on the buffet table warm.

- Ideally, drinks should be stationed at a separate table to avoid delays in the buffet line.

Poppy Seed Spinach Salad

To prepare dressing, pour vinegar and oil in blender. Add poppy seeds, sugar, minced Bermuda onion, salt, and dry mustard. Whirl for a few seconds to blend. Or place ingredients in a pint jar and shake. Refrigerate. Flavor improves if dressing is made several hours in advance.

To prepare salad, wash spinach. Dry it thoroughly and discard stems. Wash and dry lettuce. Tear spinach and lettuce in pieces into a large salad bowl. Add Swiss cheese, cottage cheese, mushrooms, and onion rings. When ready to serve, pour dressing over salad and toss to coat greens. Serve immediately. Makes 8 servings.

DRESSING

½ cup red wine vinegar

¾ cup salad oil

2 teaspoons poppy seeds

4 tablespoons sugar

1 tablespoon minced Bermuda onion

1 teaspoon salt

½ teaspoon dry mustard

SALAD

1 pound fresh spinach

½ head iceberg lettuce

1 cup shredded Swiss cheese

1 cup cottage cheese or ricotta cheese

½ pound fresh mushrooms, cleaned and sliced

½ Bermuda onion, sliced thin and

Apple Salad

Combine apples, celery, dates, nuts, and lemon juice. Sprinkle with sugar; toss and chill. Serve on lettuce leaf; garnish with cherries and Miracle Whip® or a dollop of whipped cream, if desired. Makes 10 to 12 servings.

8 tart apples, peeled (if desired) and chopped

½ cup celery, diced

½ cup dates, chopped

½ cup nuts, chopped

2 tablespoons lemon juice

2 tablespoons sugar

lettuce leaves

maraschino cherries (optional)

Miracle Whip® or whipped cream (optional)

ROLLS

1 tablespoon yeast

pinch of sugar

¼ cup water

¼ cup milk

1 tablespoon butter

½ cup sugar

½ teaspoon salt

3 eggs, beaten

4 cups all-purpose flour

ORANGE SUGAR MIXTURE

½ cup softened butter or margarine

½ cup sugar

grated peel from 1 large orange

Hot Orange Rolls

Hot Orange Rolls

Dissolve yeast and pinch of sugar in ¼ cup water. Set aside. In a small saucepan, heat milk, butter, sugar, and salt until butter is melted. Cool to lukewarm and transfer to bowl. Beat in yeast mixture, eggs, and 1 cup of the flour. Let rise until bubbly. Gradually add remaining flour and beat well with spoon or mixer. (It is not necessary to knead.) Cover and let rise until dough doubles in bulk.

In a medium bowl, mix butter, sugar, and grated orange peel; set aside. Roll dough out on lightly floured surface into rectangle and spread with the orange sugar mixture, reserving a little to sprinkle over rolls when done. Roll up as for cinnamon rolls. Cut into slices and place in greased muffin tins. Let rise until double in size. Bake at 375° for 15 to 20 minutes. Sprinkle with reserved sugar mixture. Makes 18 rolls.

Chiffon Cake

Preheat oven to 325°. Sift sugar, baking powder, flour, and salt together in a mixing bowl. Add oil, egg yolks, water, vanilla, and lemon rind to the dry ingredients. Beat until smooth. Beat egg whites in a separate bowl with cream of tartar until they form stiff peaks. Pour yolk mixture over whipped whites, folding together until blended. Bake in an ungreased 10-inch tube pan for 55 minutes, then increase temperature to 350° and bake for an additional 10 to 15 minutes. When cake tests done, invert the tube pan and let hang until cool. Glaze with lemon butter glaze, if desired.

To make lemon butter glaze, heat milk and butter together in a small saucepan. Stir in powdered sugar and mix until smooth. Add lemon juice and lemon rind; beat until shiny. Add a drop or two more liquid if needed to make desired consistency. Makes about ½ cup, or enough to glaze the top of a cake baked in a 10-inch tube pan, an 8- or 9-inch square pan, or a 9x13-inch loaf pan.

Chiffon Cake

CAKE

1¼ cups sugar

3 teaspoons baking powder

2¼ cups cake flour

1 teaspoon salt

½ cup oil

5 egg yolks

¾ cup water

2 teaspoons vanilla

2 teaspoons grated lemon rind (optional)

1 cup egg whites (7 or 8 large eggs)

½ teaspoon cream of tartar

LEMON BUTTER GLAZE

1½ tablespoons milk

1 tablespoon butter

1¼ cups powdered sugar

1 tablespoon lemon juice

½ teaspoon grated lemon rind

CHICKEN

4 whole chicken breasts, halved

4 slices Swiss cheese

8 thin slices cooked ham*

salt and pepper

thyme or rosemary

¼ cup melted butter or margarine

½ cup corn flake crumbs

CORDON BLEU SAUCE

1 10½-ounce can cream
of chicken soup

½ cup sour cream

juice of 1 lemon

e

1 cup milk

½ cup bread crumbs

2 pounds lean ground beef

2 eggs, lightly beaten

¼ cup onion, grated

3 tablespoons fresh parsley,
chopped

1 tablespoon salt

¼ teaspoon allspice

1 cup beef broth or bouillon

Chicken Cordon Bleu

Skin and bone chicken breast halves. Place each half between sheets of plastic wrap and pound with meat mallet to about ⅛-inch thick.

Cut Swiss cheese into fingers about 1½ inches long and ½ inch thick. On each ham slice place a finger of cheese. Sprinkle lightly with seasonings. Roll ham and cheese jelly-roll style, then roll each chicken breast with ham and cheese inside. Tuck in ends and seal well. (Tie roll if necessary, or fasten edges with toothpicks.) Dip each roll in melted butter, then roll in corn flake crumbs, turning to thoroughly coat each roll.

Place rolls in a 9x13x2-inch baking dish. Bake, uncovered, at 400° for about 40 minutes, or until chicken is golden brown. Serve with cordon bleu sauce, if desired. Makes 6 to 8 servings.

To make sauce, blend together soup, sour cream, and lemon; heat. Serve over chicken. Makes about 2 cups.

Baked or boiled ham slices may be used.

Swedish Meatballs

Pour milk in a large bowl, stir in crumbs, and let soak for a few minutes. Add ground beef, eggs, onion, parsley, salt, and allspice. Mix together and shape into 36 small balls.

Put meatballs into a large frying pan and cook over medium heat until they are browned on all sides. Pour beef broth over meatballs and simmer, covered, for 15 minutes. Makes 12 servings of 3 meatballs each.

Swedish Meatballs, Vegetable Medley, Rice with Mushrooms

Rice with Mushrooms

¼ cup butter

1 onion, minced

6 to 8 mushrooms, thinly sliced

1 cup converted rice

2 10½-ounce cans beef consommé

1 10½-ounce can cream of mushroom soup

Preheat oven to 325°. Melt butter in medium-size sauté pan. Sauté minced onion and mushrooms over medium heat until onions are translucent and mushrooms are soft. Remove to mixing bowl and add rice, beef consommé, and soup. Stir well. Pour in 9x9-inch casserole dish and bake for 1½ hours.

Marinated Tomato Slices

3 large tomatoes, sliced

olive oil

3 tablespoons fresh basil

½ teaspoon salt

¼ teaspoon freshly ground pepper

Place sliced tomatoes in large bowl; cover with olive oil. Combine basil, salt, and pepper; sprinkle over tomatoes, and toss to blend well. Cover and refrigerate for several hours. Drain tomatoes, reserving marinade if desired for future use with meat or other vegetables. Serve tomatoes cold. Makes 6 servings.

Marinated Tomato Slices

Vegetable Medley

2 medium carrots

3 small zucchini

3 ribs of celery

2 tablespoons butter

salt and pepper to taste

Peel carrots; clean zucchini and celery. Slice vegetables on the diagonal. Bring ¼ inch water to a boil and add butter. Add the carrots and simmer, covered, for 4 minutes. Add the celery and simmer an additional 2 minutes. Add the zucchini and continue cooking for an additional 5 minutes, or until all vegetables are tender-crisp. Season to taste with salt and pepper. Serve at once, retaining the remaining liquid in the serving dish. Makes 4 servings.

Sarah's Salad

Wash and drain lettuce. Dry thoroughly. Dice bacon and sauté until crisp; drain on paper towels. Run hot water over frozen peas and drain. Tear lettuce in bite-size pieces into salad bowl. Sprinkle with sugar, salt, and pepper. Add peas, cheese, green onion, mayonnaise, and salad dressing. (These ingredients may be layered, if desired, with the mayonnaise spread on last.) Chill. Toss when ready to serve and garnish with bacon. Makes 8 servings.

* 2½ ounces Swiss cheese cut into strips may be substituted.

1 head iceberg lettuce

3 strips bacon

½ 10-ounce package frozen peas

¼ teaspoon sugar

½ teaspoon salt

¼ teaspoon pepper

½ cup Swiss cheese, shredded*

⅔ cup green onion, chopped

¼ cup mayonnaise

¼ cup salad dressing

Sarah's Salad

Coleslaw Cardinal

Toss grapes and cabbage together; cover and chill. Combine orange juice and water in a small saucepan; blend in cornstarch, mustard, and salt. Cook, stirring constantly, over medium heat until mixture boils. Stir a small amount of hot mixture quickly into egg; return egg mixture to pan. Add hot pepper sauce.

Cook over low heat, stirring constantly, until dressing thickens; remove from heat and blend in lemon juice. Allow to cool; cover and refrigerate until serving time. When ready to serve, blend sour cream into dressing; toss lightly with grapes and cabbage. Makes 8 servings.

3½ cups red seedless grapes, halved

3½ cups finely shredded cabbage

⅓ cup frozen orange juice concentrate, thawed

⅓ cup water

2 tablespoons cornstarch

prepared mustard to taste

½ teaspoon salt

1 egg, beaten

dash of hot pepper sauce

2 tablespoons lemon juice

½ cup sour cream

Lion House Dinner Rolls

See recipe on page 57.

Pecan Bars

Make the topping first and allow it to cool while preparing and baking the crust. To make the topping, mix butter, brown sugar, and honey in a saucepan over medium heat. Bring to a boil and cook until it has boiled 5 minutes, stirring constantly. Remove from heat. Cool slightly and add cream and pecans.

To make crust, preheat oven to 375°. Grease a 9x13-inch cake pan. In a large mixing bowl, cream butter and sugar. Add eggs and lemon rind; beat until smooth. Add flour and baking powder and mix well. Press the dough into the bottom of the pan, pricking evenly with a fork. Bake 12 to 15 minutes or until dough looks half done. (Overbaking at this point will cause the crust to be too hard by the time the second baking is complete.) Reduce heat to 350°. Spread topping evenly over the partially baked crust and bake for an additional 30 to 35 minutes, or until topping is set. Cut into bars. Makes about 15 to 24 bars, depending on the size of the bars.

TOPPING

1½ cups butter

1½ cups brown sugar

1½ cups honey

½ cup heavy whipping cream

4 cups pecans

CRUST

1 cup butter

1 cup sugar

3 eggs

grated rind of 1 lemon

4 cups all-purpose flour

½ teaspoon baking powder

Pecan Bars

Cream Cheese Brownies

Follow package directions for cake-like brownies; place in a 9x9-inch pan. In a separate bowl, combine cream cheese and sugar until creamy. Add egg and milk; mix until smooth. Drop cream cheese batter onto the brownie batter by teaspoonfuls and swirl. Bake for 35 to 40 minutes. Cut into 3-inch squares. Makes 9 brownies.

Lemon Bars

To make crust, preheat oven to 350°. Put butter in mixing bowl and beat until softened. Add flour and powdered sugar and mix on low speed until just combined. Spread dough evenly in a 9x13-inch pan. Bake for 10 minutes or until the corners are light golden brown. Remove from oven.

To make filling, mix together eggs, sugar, lemon juice, flour, and baking powder in a medium bowl. Mix with a wire whisk or with a mixer set on low speed for just a few minutes. (It is important not to mix a lot of air into the filling.) Pour on top of partially baked crust and bake at 350° for 30 to 35 minutes. Allow to cool slightly and dust with powdered sugar before cutting into bars. Makes 18 to 24 bars.

---

1 package deluxe brownie mix

1 8-ounce package cream cheese, softened

⅓ cup sugar

1 egg

2 tablespoons milk

CRUST

1¼ cups butter

2¼ cups all-purpose flour

½ cup powdered sugar

FILLING

4 eggs

2 cups sugar

6 tablespoons lemon juice

4 tablespoons all-purpose flour

1 teaspoon baking powder

Prime Rib, Boston Brown Oven-Roasted
Potatoes, and Asparagus with Hollandaise

8

Whether entertaining family, friends, or business associates, a sit-down dinner party no longer requires a formal table. It should, however, consist of a fairly substantial menu of multiple courses with ample time to savor and appreciate the food. The most common kind of at-home entertaining, a formal dinner allows time for long, old-fashioned conversations and time to establish or renew friendships. Often, however, a memorable meal can leave the cook too busy to join family and friends. Choose elegantly simple recipes that can be completely or partially prepared ahead, and then enjoy the evening.

Formal Dinners

Poppy Seed Spinach Salad

Lemon Ice

Cornmeal Rolls

Pork Tenderloin with Baked Apples

Old-Fashioned Mashed Potatoes

Broccoli Spears

Meltdown Chocolate Cake

~

Orange, Grapefruit, and Avocado Salad

French Onion Soup

Whole Wheat Roll

Lion House Chicken

Rice Pilaf

Sautéed Summer Squash Medley

Very Berry Pie a la Mode

~

Shrimp Cocktail

Gazpacho

Spring Mix Salad

Pineapple Sorbet

Lion House Dinner Rolls

Prime Rib

Boston Brown Oven-Roasted Potatoes

Asparagus with Hollandaise

Baked Alaska

Poppy Seed Spinach Salad

See recipe on page 69.

12 large lemons

2 envelopes unflavored gelatin

2 cups sugar

4½ cups water

mint sprigs for garnish

Lemon Ice

Squeeze the juice from all lemons. It should yield approximately 1½ cups juice. Grate peel of 4 lemons.

In a 1-quart saucepan over low heat, cook gelatin, sugar, and water, stirring constantly, until gelatin is dissolved. Remove pan from heat and stir in lemon juice and grated lemon peel.

Pour mixture into a 9x13-inch baking pan. Cover and freeze about 3 hours until partially frozen. Spoon lemon mixture into large chilled mixing bowl. With mixer at medium speed, beat until smooth but still frozen. Return mixture to baking pan; cover and freeze about 2 hours or until partially frozen. As before, spoon mixture into chilled large bowl and mix with mixer at medium speed, beating until smooth but still frozen. Return to pan and freeze until firm.

Just before serving, let the ice stand at room temperature for 10 minutes. Scoop into chilled dessert cups and garnish with mint sprigs. Makes 8 to 10 servings.

Tips and Ideas

- Consider seating a large group in the family room or living room if the dining room is too small.

- The host should plan the seating for a formal dinner, but place cards are only necessary for large groups or events where guests cannot be easily directed to a specific table or seat.

- Serve ices or sorbets in large, hollowed-out lemons on doily lined dessert plates. Garnish with mint or lemon leaves.

- When planning color schemes, remember that a monochromatic effect can be particularly elegant. Use colors of the same hue in linens, table settings, flowers, centerpiece, and decorations. An all-white theme can be especially elegant.

Cornmeal Rolls

In a double boiler, combine milk, melted shortening, sugar, cornmeal, and salt. Cook, stirring frequently, until the mixture is thick. Cool to lukewarm. Dissolve yeast in ¼ cup lukewarm water. Add the yeast mixture and the eggs to the cornmeal mixture and beat well.

Let rise in a greased bowl for 2 hours, then add the flour to form a soft dough. Knead lightly. Roll out dough on a floured surface and cut in with a biscuit cutter. Brush the dough pieces with melted butter, then crease them and fold in half. Place on a greased cookie sheet. Let rise for 1 hour. Bake at 375° for 15 minutes. Makes 3 dozen rolls.

2 cups milk

½ cup shortening, melted

½ cup sugar

½ cup cornmeal

I teaspoon salt

I package active dry yeast

¼ cup lukewarm water

2 eggs, beaten

4 cups all-purpose flour

melted butter

Pork Tenderloin with Baked Apples

Place pork in roasting pan. Make seasoning by mixing together salt, garlic salt, seasoning salt, pepper, and rosemary. Lightly sprinkle seasoning mixture over pork. Cook in preheated oven at 350° for about 30 minutes or until brown, then add 1 cup water. Cover with foil and cook for another 1½ hours at 225°. Pull out of oven and let sit about 10 minutes before slicing.

To make gravy, drain meat juices into pot. In a bowl, mix together ½ cup water and cornstarch until smooth. Slowly add to pork juices, stirring constantly over medium-low heat. To thicken gravy, add more cornstarch mixture until gravy reaches desired consistency.

To make baked apples, lay apple slices on greased sheet pan. Sprinkle with brown sugar first, then dribble with melted butter. Cook in preheated oven at 325° for about 15 minutes or until brown.

Serve pork slices with baked apples and gravy. Makes 12 servings.

PORK

5 pounds pork tenderloin

SEASONING MIX

I teaspoon salt

⅛ teaspoon garlic salt

⅛ teaspoon seasoning salt

dash black pepper

½ teaspoon rosemary

I cup water

GRAVY

juices from cooked pork

½ cup water

2 tablespoons cornstarch

BAKED APPLES

4 Granny Smith apples, sliced

I cup brown sugar

4 tablespoons butter, melted

Old-Fashioned Mashed Potatoes

12 medium potatoes

1 teaspoon salt

4 tablespoons butter

¼ to ½ cup half-and-half

Peel and quarter potatoes. Cover with cold water. Sprinkle with salt. Bring to a rapid boil; cook over medium heat until tender. Drain water and add butter and half-and-half; beat with electric beater or handheld potato masher until light and fluffy. Place in serving bowl and serve hot. Makes 10 to 12 servings.

Meltdown Chocolate Cake

CAKE

¾ cup semi-sweet chocolate chips

½ cup butter

¼ cup cake flour, stirred before measuring

½ cup sugar

3 eggs

FROSTING

¼ cup whipping cream

1 teaspoon butter

½ cup semi-sweet chocolate chips

In a heavy saucepan over medium heat, melt chocolate chips and butter.

In a large mixing bowl, combine cake flour, sugar, and eggs. Mix until blended. With mixer at high speed, pour in the chocolate mixture. Beat on high speed for 5 minutes until batter is light. Scrape sides of bowl often.

Butter a 9-inch springform pan and dust with sugar. Pour chocolate mixture into pan. Bake at 400° for 15 to 20 minutes or until a toothpick inserted in center comes out clean. Loosen side with knife. Invert onto cooling rack over a sheet of wax paper. Let cool.

To make frosting, boil whipping cream in a saucepan for 1 minute, stirring constantly. Remove from heat and stir in butter and remaining chocolate chips. Spread over top and sides of cake. Makes 16 servings.

Tips and Ideas

• Individual centerpieces give each place setting a personal touch. Consider a small wrapped gift, a miniature vase with a single bud, or a piece of fruit tied with a beautiful ribbon.

• Every recipe is made instantly more appealing when garnished or decorated. Easy-to-make garnishes include a sprig of parsley, chopped fresh herbs, cucumber twists, carrot curls, stuffed olives, cheese shavings, lemon or lime slices, curled orange peelings, nuts, chocolate shavings or sprinkles, and cinnamon sticks.

• A translucent colored-glass vase, particularly in an Art Nouveau style, makes an elegant and interesting water pitcher.

Pork Tenderloin with Baked Apples, Broccoli Spears, Old-Fashioned Mashed Potatoes, and Meltdown Chocolate Cake

CATALINA DRESSING

1 cup vinegar

1 cup salad oil

1 cup sugar

1 cup ketchup

2 teaspoons salt

1½ teaspoons garlic powder

1 tablespoon fresh white
onion, minced

SALAD

4 large oranges

2 ripe avocados

2 cans grapefruit

3 cans Mandarin oranges

1 head of butter lettuce

❧

3 large white onions, sliced

⅓ cup butter or margarine

3 14-ounce cans Swanson®
beef broth

1¼ teaspoons salt

¼ teaspoon garlic powder

3 tablespoons grated
Parmesan cheese

8 to 12 slices baguette-style
French bread

2 cups Swiss cheese, grated

2 cups mozzarella cheese, grated

½ cup Parmesan cheese, shredded

Orange, Grapefruit, and Avocado Salad

To make dressing, put vinegar, oil, sugar, ketchup, salt, garlic powder, and onion in a jar and shake well. Chill for a few hours. Shake again just before serving.

To prepare fruit, peel and section oranges. Peel, pit, and slice avocados. Open cans of grapefruit and Mandarin oranges and drain. Arrange butter lettuce leaves on plates. Arrange avocados and fruit on top of lettuce. Drizzle dressing over salad before serving.

Orange, Grapefruit, and Avocado Salad

French Onion Soup

Sauté onions in melted butter in a large saucepan over medium heat for 15 to 20 minutes or until onions begin to turn transparent. Add beef broth, salt, and garlic powder to onions. Bring mixture to a boil, then reduce heat and simmer uncovered for 1 hour. Add the grated Parmesan cheese after the mixture has simmered for 50 minutes.

When soup is done, preheat oven to 350°. Toast bread for 10 minutes or until golden brown. Remove bread from oven and turn oven to broil.

Prepare each serving of soup by spooning about 1 cup of soup into an oven-safe bowl. Float a toasted slice or two of bread on top of the soup, then sprinkle ⅓ cup of the Swiss cheese and ⅓ cup of the mozzarella cheese on top of the bread. Add a sprinkle of shredded Parmesan cheese on each.

Place the bowl on a baking sheet and broil for about 5 minutes or until the cheeses are melted and start to brown. Makes 6 servings.

Whole Wheat Rolls

Instructions for Mixing with Electric Mixer

In a large mixing bowl, soften yeast in 3 cups lukewarm water until dissolved. Add remaining ingredients and beat until dough forms a ball and leaves sides of bowl (part of the flour may need to be mixed in by hand). Remove beaters, cover bowl, and let dough rise for 1 hour in warm area away from drafts. Pinch 1¼-inch pieces and place on a greased cookie sheet 1½ inches apart. Let rise until they double in size (30 to 40 minutes). Bake at 375° for 12 to 15 minutes. Makes 4 dozen rolls.

Instructions for Hand Mixing

Dissolve yeast in ¼ cup of the lukewarm water. In a large mixing bowl, combine remaining 2¾ cups water, oatmeal, molasses, and nonfat dry milk; add half of the white flour and half of the whole wheat flour, one cup at a time, beating well after each addition. Add dissolved yeast, the remaining flour, shortening, and salt. Mix well, then knead until dough is smooth and elastic. Place in a covered bowl in a warm area until dough has doubled in bulk. Knead for one minute to force out air bubbles. Pinch 1¼-inch pieces and place on a greased cookie sheet 1½ inches apart. Let rise until they double in size (30 to 40 minutes). Bake at 375° for 12 to 15 minutes. Makes 4 dozen rolls.

1 package active dry yeast

3 cups lukewarm water

1 cup oatmeal

¼ cup molasses

6 tablespoons nonfat dry milk

1 cup white flour

6½ cups whole wheat flour

6 tablespoons shortening, softened

1½ tablespoons salt

Lion House Chicken

Lay whole chicken breasts flat on baking sheet. Coat with bread crumbs. Prepare your favorite stuffing with mushrooms and butter. Portion stuffing mixture into 10 to 12 equal parts. Put stuffing on one half of each chicken breast; fold over and secure with toothpicks. Bake at 375° for 30 minutes. Makes 10 to 12 servings.

To make sauce, mix honey, mayonnaise, and mustard together in a small saucepan and heat over medium heat until warmed through. Top each cooked chicken breast with sauce before serving.

CHICKEN

10 to 12 8-ounce boneless, skinless chicken breasts

2 cups ground bread crumbs

4 cups favorite stuffing mix

1 cup mushrooms, sliced

1 cup butter, melted

DIJON MUSTARD SAUCE

½ cup honey

2 cups mayonnaise

⅓ cup Dijon mustard

Rice Pilaf

See recipe on page 61.

Sautéed Summer Squash Medley

1 large onion

3 small yellow summer squash

3 small zucchini

1 red pepper

1 green pepper

1 yellow or orange pepper

2 tablespoons olive oil

1 teaspoon oregano

1 teaspoon basil

2 teaspoons salt

1 cup pitted sliced black olives

1 cup crumbled ricotta cheese
or 1 cup crumbled mildly
herbed goat cheese

1 tablespoon freshly squeezed
lemon juice

Clean and slice onion, squash, zucchini, and peppers. Heat oil in a skillet; sauté onion until transparent. Add squash, zucchini, and pepers; stir fry until tender-crisp, which will take about 4 minutes on medium heat. Add oregano, basil, and salt. Toss with olives, cheese, and lemon juice. Makes 8 servings.

Rice Pilaf and Sautéed Summer Squash Medley

Very Berry Pie a la Mode

Thaw all berries, then pour berries and all of the juice in a mixing bowl. In a separate bowl, mix together sugar, salt, and cornstarch; pour on top of berries. Mix well with a rubber spatula. Fill crusts; add top crusts and bake at 375° for 45 to 50 minutes or until golden brown. Top each serving of pie with a large scoop of vanilla ice cream. Makes 2 pies.

pastry for two 2-crust pies

1 16-ounce bag frozen boysenberries (no sugar added)

1 8-ounce bag frozen blueberries (no sugar added)

1 8-ounce bag frozen raspberries (no sugar added)

1¾ cups sugar

½ teaspoon salt

½ cup cornstarch

Shrimp Cocktail

To make cocktail sauce, mix together chili sauce, horseradish, chives, lemon juice, and Tabasco sauce, if desired. Let sit for 2 hours.

Slice lettuce, green onions, and celery very thin, then toss together. Place lettuce mixture into individual dishes; add the bay shrimp on top of the lettuce. Place the fantail shrimp around the bay shrimp. Cut lemons into wedges, and garnish each dish with a lemon wedge on the side. Top with cocktail sauce, or serve it on the side. Makes 12 servings.

COCKTAIL SAUCE

3 cups chili sauce

½ tablespoon horseradish

½ teaspoon chives

½ teaspoon lemon juice

2 or 3 drops Tabasco sauce (optional)

SHRIMP SALAD

1 head iceberg lettuce

¼ cup green onions

½ cup celery

2 pounds bay shrimp

3 pounds fantail shrimp

3 lemons

Tips and Ideas

- Between courses, clear plates two by two or with the aid of a tray, as inconspicuously as possible. Enlist the help of your spouse or a friend, but avoid having everyone get up to clear plates.

- For a glorious dessert presentation, fill a squeeze bottle with raspberry, caramel, or chocolate sauce and drizzle a quick pattern across individual plates.

4 ripe tomatoes, peeled
and quartered

½ large green pepper, seeded
and sliced

½ small onion, peeled and sliced

1 cucumber, peeled and sliced

1 clove garlic, minced

1 teaspoon salt

¼ teaspoon pepper

2 tablespoons olive oil

3 tablespoons vinegar

½ cup ice water

SALAD

1 head red leaf lettuce, washed
and broken into pieces

1 head romaine lettuce, washed
and broken into pieces

½ package spinach, with
stems trimmed

2 Fuji apples, cored and cut
into bite-size pieces

½ cup green grapes

½ cup red grapes

1 cup sugared almonds

DRESSING

⅔ cup orange juice

4 tablespoons red wine vinegar

4 tablespoons sugar

⅔ cup oil

2 tablespoons dry Good Seasons®
Italian dressing mix

Gazpacho

Place half of each of the ingredients in one bowl; place the second half in a separate bowl. Fill blender container with ingredients from one bowl. Cover and blend for just 2 seconds; pour back into bowl. Repeat with ingredients from second bowl. Combine both bowls of blended gazpacho and chill in refrigerator. Or pour into soup plates and serve with an ice cube in the center of each serving. Makes 6 servings.

Spring Mix Salad

In a large serving bowl, combine lettuces, spinach, apples, and grapes; toss. To make dressing, combine orange juice, vinegar, sugar, oil, and dry Italian seasonings mix; mix well. Toss enough of the dressing into the salad to coat the ingredients lightly. Add almonds last. Makes 12 servings.

Gazpacho

Pineapple Sorbet

In a 1-quart saucepan over medium heat, bring sugar and water to boiling, stirring the mixture constantly. Remove from heat and set aside.

With a sharp knife, cut crown and stems off pineapple; cut off rinds. Cut pineapple in half and remove core, then cut pineapple into small pieces.

In a covered blender at medium speed, blend pineapple until smooth. Strain into a large bowl; use a spoon to press out all the juice. Discard fibers. Stir sugar mixture and lemon juice into pineapple.

In a small bowl with mixer at high speed, beat egg whites into stiff peaks. Add vanilla. Fold beaten egg whites into pineapple mixture. Pour into 13x9-inch baking pan. Cover with foil and freeze for about 3½ hours, or until firm.

Spoon pineapple mixture into chilled large bowl; with mixer at low speed, beat until softened. Increase speed to medium and beat until fluffy but still frozen; return to baking pan. Cover with foil. Freeze 2 hours until partially frozen. Spoon into chilled large bowl and beat again as above. Return mixture to baking pan; cover again with foil and freeze until firm.

When ready to serve, let sorbet sit at room temperature for about 10 minutes. Scoop into serving dishes. Makes 6 servings.

Note: When making this recipe begin early in the day or a day ahead.

¾ cup sugar

½ cup water

1 large pineapple

3 tablespoons lemon juice

2 egg whites, at room temperature

¼ teaspoon vanilla

Lion House Dinner Rolls

See recipe on page 57.

cut of prime rib beef

coarse black pepper

kosher salt

garlic powder

Prime Rib, Boston Brown Oven-Roasted
Potatoes, and Asparagus with Hollandaise

8 potatoes, peeled and parboiled

½ cup butter or margarine, melted

1 tablespoon paprika

2 teaspoons salt

1 tablespoon seasoned salt

½ teaspoon pepper

Prime Rib

Consult your local butcher in advance for advice on purchase weight and yield for a cut of prime rib beef.

Preheat oven to 280°. Generously season the prime rib with pepper, salt, and garlic powder. Put prime rib, fat side up, in a heavy, deep roasting pan. Put in oven and bake for 1½ hours. Turn the roasting pan a quarter turn and cook for another 1½ hours. Make a final ¼ turn, cook approximately 30 to 40 minutes more, then check internal temperature, using a quick-read thermometer. If the temperature reads 145°, the roast will be medium rare. Cook longer if medium or well-done roast is desired. A thermometer reading of 156° will be medium, and 165° will be well-done.

Turn oven down to 165° and leave door partially open. Let prime rib sit for 30 minutes before slicing. It is very important to let the roast rest at 165° before slicing.

Carefully remove pan from oven; place roast on cutting board. Slice to desired thickness and serve.

Boston Brown Oven-Roasted Potatoes

Peel and boil potatoes until tender-crisp. Cut into chunks and place in a shallow baking dish or on a baking sheet. Pour melted butter over potatoes and stir until well coated. Sprinkle paprika, salt, seasoned salt, and pepper over all and bake at 400° for about 15 minutes or until lightly brown and crisp on top. Makes 8 to 10 servings.

Asparagus with Hollandaise

Steam the asparagus while you are making the hollandaise sauce.

Begin making sauce 15 minutes before you want to serve it. Put egg yolks and lemon juice in the top of a double boiler. With a wire whisk, beat until well mixed. Put hot water, *not boiling,* in bottom part of double boiler. Place the top of the double boiler over the bottom, add one half of the butter to the egg yolk mixture. Cook, beating constantly, until the butter is completely melted. Add the remaining half of the butter, beating until the mixture thickens and is heated through.

Remove from heat; stir in salt. Keep warm. Serve over asparagus. Makes 6 to 8 servings.

2 pounds fresh asparagus

3 egg yolks

2 tablespoons lemon juice

½ cup butter

¼ teaspoon salt

Baked Alaska

Spoon ice cream into pie shell. Drizzle with chocolate syrup and place in freezer until ready to use.

Heat oven to 500°. To make meringue, beat together egg whites, vanilla, and cream of tartar until foamy. Gradually beat in sugar until mixture is stiff and glossy. Completely cover ice cream in pie shell with meringue, sealing well to edge of crust and piling high. (If desired, pie may be frozen up to 24 hours at this point.)

When ready to serve, bake pie on lowest oven rack for 3 to 5 minutes or until meringue is light brown. Serve immediately (or again return to freezer until ready to serve). Makes 6 to 8 servings.

PIE

baked 8-inch pie shell

1 quart peppermint ice cream

2 to 3 tablespoons chocolate syrup

MERINGUE

5 egg whites

1 teaspoon vanilla

½ teaspoon cream of tartar

⅔ cup sugar

Crown Roast of Pork, Fresh String Green Beans,
Oven-Baked Mashed Potatoes, and Lion House Dinner Roll

Holiday Dinners

9

Whether the occasion is Thanksgiving, Christmas, or Easter, holidays are a time for festive entertaining on a grand scale. Sharing important occasions with family and friends can create memories and traditions that will endure for generations. Capture the magic of the season with tempting food, lovely table settings, and creative table decorations. Colorful autumn leaves, nuts and pinecones, candles of all shapes and sizes, fresh flowers such as bright white tulips or burgundy calla lilies, sugared fruits, or glass ornaments are only a few of the many decorations that will add a festive flair to your holiday meal.

Sour Cream Yogurt Rolls

Blueberry Salad

Sesame Seed Asparagus

Sweet Potato Bake

Perfect Parsley Potatoes

Baked Holiday Ham or
Baked Ham with Red Currant Sauce

Lemon Cream Pie

❧

Quick Potato Rolls

Parsley Buttered Carrots

Apple Walnut Salad

Whipped Sweet Potato Bake

Old-Fashioned Mashed Potatoes

Old-Fashioned Gravy

Cranberry Orange Relish or
Cranberry Raspberry Chutney

Roast Turkey

Pecan Corn Bread Stuffing

Pumpkin Pie or Raisin Cream Pie

❧

Lion House Dinner Rolls

Fresh String Green Beans

Crunchy Apple Salad

Candied Yam Soufflé

Oven-Baked Mashed Potatoes

Crown Roast of Pork

Roasted Cashew Stuffing

Christmas Pudding

Sour Cream Yogurt Rolls

1¼ cups whole wheat flour, divided

3½ cups all-purpose flour, divided

2 packages active dry yeast

2 teaspoons salt

½ teaspoon baking soda

½ cup sour cream

1 cup plain yogurt

½ cup water

3 tablespoons butter

2 tablespoons honey

In a mixing bowl, combine whole wheat flour, 1 cup of all-purpose flour, yeast, salt, and baking soda. In a saucepan over low heat, heat sour cream, yogurt, water, butter, and honey to 130°. Pour over dry ingredients and blend well, then beat on medium speed for 3 minutes. Add enough of the remaining all-purpose flour to form soft dough.

Turn onto a floured surface; knead until smooth and elastic, about 6 to 8 minutes. Place in a greased bowl turning once to grease top. Cover and let rise in a warm place until double in size, about 1 hour.

Punch dough down; divide into 24 pieces. Roll each piece into a 9-inch rope. Form "S" shaped rolls by coiling each end of rope toward center in opposite directions until dough is shaped like the letter "S." Place 3 inches apart on greased baking sheets. Cover and let rise until double in size, about 30 minutes. Bake at 400° for 15 minutes or until golden brown. Spray tops with nonstick cooking spray while warm. Cool on wire racks. Makes 2 dozen rolls.

Blueberry Salad

1 6-ounce package raspberry gelatin

2 cups boiling water

8 ounces cream cheese

1 15-ounce can blueberries, with syrup

1 15-ounce can crushed pineapple, drained

1 pint whipping cream

red leaf lettuce

fresh blueberries

Dissolve raspberry gelatin in 2 cups boiling water. Dissolve cream cheese in hot gelatin. Add blueberries and crushed pineapple. Whip the cream and fold into gelatin mixture, reserving some for garnish. Spread mixture into a 9x13-inch pan and refrigerate until set.

When ready to serve, wash lettuce and dry thoroughly. Wash blueberries and set aside. Put a leaf of red leaf lettuce on each individual salad plate. Cut blueberry salad into squares and put individual portions on lettuce. Garnish with fresh blueberries and a dollop of whipped cream. Makes 10 to 12 servings.

Sesame Seed Asparagus

Place asparagus spears in a large skillet; add boiling water and salt. Cook over medium-high heat for 5 to 7 minutes or until tender. Remove asparagus and keep warm. Drain cooking liquid, reserving ½ cup in a small saucepan. In a small bowl, combine cornstarch and cold water; stir into liquid. Cook and stir over medium heat until thickened and bubbly; cook 1 minute more, stirring constantly. Add butter and stir until melted. Spoon sauce over asparagus; sprinkle with sesame seeds and serve immediately. Makes 6 to 8 servings.

2 pounds fresh asparagus

1 cup boiling water

½ teaspoon salt

1 tablespoon cornstarch

¼ cup cold water

¼ cup butter

3 tablespoons sesame seeds, toasted

Sweet Potato Bake

In a greased 11x7x2-inch baking pan, arrange sweet potatoes and apple slices. In a small saucepan, combine brown sugar, cornstarch, and salt. Add apricot nectar, orange juice, water, and orange peel; stir until blended. Add butter. Bring to a boil over medium-high heat; turn heat down to medium and stir for 2 minutes or until thickened. Stir in pecans. Pour over sweet potatoes and apples. Cover and bake at 375° for 35 minutes. Makes 6 servings.

4 cups cooked sweet potato wedges, steamed or boiled

1 medium tart apple, peeled and thinly sliced

½ cup light brown sugar

2¼ teaspoons cornstarch

⅛ teaspoon salt

¼ cup apricot nectar

¼ cup freshly squeezed orange juice

¼ cup water

1 teaspoon orange peel

1 tablespoon butter

¼ cup pecans

Tips and Ideas

• Resist the temptation to try an entire menu of new recipes for a special event. Stick with one or two new dishes, particularly if you don't have time for a trial run.

• Make your holiday less stressful by planning a progressive dinner. Have appetizers at one home, the main course at another, and dessert at a third.

• Save some last-minute preparation tasks for helpful guests who want to join you in the kitchen. Remember to have an extra apron or two on hand.

Perfect Parsley Potatoes

2 pounds small red potatoes

½ cup butter

¼ cup fresh parsley, chopped

¼ teaspoon dried marjoram

Cook whole potatoes in boiling salted water for 15 minutes or until tender. Cool slightly. With a sharp knife, remove one narrow strip of skin around the middle of each potato. In a large skillet, melt butter; add parsley and marjoram. Add the potatoes and stir gently until coated and heated through. Makes 6 to 8 servings.

Baked Holiday Ham

1 uncooked smoked ham with bone (12 pounds)

1 jar Dijon mustard with whole seeds

2 cups apricot marmalade

¾ cup apple juice

Preheat oven to 250°. Line a baking pan with foil. Put the ham on the foil, fat side up. Wrap well with another piece of foil. Bake for 3½ hours. Remove from oven, unwrap, and with a large, sharp knife cut off the rind and all but about ¼ inch of fat. Score the fat in a diamond pattern, making the lines ¾-inch apart.

Combine mustard, marmalade, and apple juice to make a glaze. Pour out any pan juices, then lightly coat the ham with the glaze and return it to the oven for an additional hour. Every 15 minutes, spoon more of the glaze over the ham. Remove to a serving platter until ready to carve. Makes 20 servings.

Baked Ham with Red Currant Sauce

HAM

1 ham with bone (8 to 10 pounds)

1 cup packed brown sugar

2 teaspoons dry mustard

whole cloves

RED CURRANT SAUCE

2 cups red currant jelly

½ cup orange juice

½ cup lemon juice

½ cup pineapple juice

4 tablespoons honey

2 tablespoons cornstarch

Remove skin from ham; score the surface with shallow diagonal cuts, making a diamond pattern. Mix brown sugar and mustard together; rub into ham. Insert a whole clove in center of each diamond. Place ham in a large roaster with a baking rack. Bake uncovered, at 325°, for 20 to 22 minutes per pound. Remove to serving platter until ready to carve.

To make red currant sauce, combine jelly, orange juice, lemon juice, pineapple juice, honey, and cornstarch in a medium saucepan. Cook over medium heat until thickened, stirring often. Serve over the sliced ham. Makes 3½ cups sauce.

Baked Ham with Red Currant Sauce, Perfect Parsley Potatoes, and Asparagus with Hollandaise*

* From the Formal Dinners chapter

Lemon Cream Pie

baked 9-inch pie shell

1¼ cups sugar

¼ teaspoon salt

6 tablespoons cornstarch

1½ cups boiling water

3 eggs, slightly beaten

6 tablespoons lemon juice

¼ teaspoon grated lemon rind

2 tablespoons butter or margarine

1 cup heavy cream, whipped
and sweetened

Combine sugar, salt, and cornstarch in a 2- or 3-quart saucepan. Blend well. Place over medium heat and add the boiling water, stirring rapidly until smooth and thick. Bring to a full boil to thoroughly cook the cornstarch. Remove from heat.

In a medium bowl, slightly beat eggs. Add a little of the hot pudding to the eggs while stirring rapidly. Pour egg mixture into hot pudding in saucepan and reheat, stirring constantly, just until smooth.

Remove from heat and add lemon juice, grated rind, and butter; stir well. Pour into baked pie shell. Cover surface with plastic wrap to prevent a skin from forming. Chill. Serve topped with whipped cream. Makes 1 pie.

Quick Potato Rolls

⅔ cup sugar

⅔ cup shortening

1 cup potato flakes

2½ teaspoons salt

2 eggs

2 packages active dry yeast

1⅓ cups warm water, divided

6 to 6½ cups all-purpose flour

In a large mixing bowl, cream sugar and shortening; set aside. Make potato flakes according to package directions. Add potatoes, salt, and eggs to creamed mixture.

In a small bowl, dissolve yeast in ⅔ cup warm water; add to creamed mixture. Beat in 2 cups flour and remaining water. Add enough remaining flour to form a soft dough. Shape into a ball; do not knead. Place in a greased bowl, turning once to grease top. Cover and let rise in a warm place until double in size, about 1 hour.

Punch dough down; divide into thirds. Shape each portion into 15 balls and arrange in three greased 9-inch round baking pans. Cover and let rise until double in size, about 30 minutes. Bake at 375° for 20 to 25 minutes. Remove from pans to cool on wire racks. Makes 45 rolls.

Parsley Buttered Carrots

In a medium saucepan, cook carrots in boiling salted water for 10 minutes or until tender. Drain water and add butter and parsley. Toss lightly until carrots are well-coated. Makes 10 to 12 servings.

2 pounds baby carrots

2 tablespoons butter, melted

1 tablespoon dried parsley

Apple Walnut Salad

In a small bowl, combine cider vinegar, olive oil, salt, and sugar; mix well. Combine apples, onion, and raisins in medium bowl. Pour vinegar mixture over apple mixture and lightly toss. Cover and let stand for 15 minutes.

Wash and dry spinach and romaine lettuce, and tear into pieces in large salad bowl. Add apple mixture and toss. Sprinkle walnuts over salad and serve. Makes 12 to 14 servings.

4 tablespoons cider vinegar

4 tablespoons olive oil

½ teaspoon salt

½ teaspoon sugar

2 cups apples, peeled and cut into ½-inch pieces

½ sweet red onion, cut into ½-inch strips

½ cup raisins

4 cups fresh spinach

4 cups romaine lettuce

½ cup walnuts, chopped

Tips and Ideas

• Holiday dinners may be served plated from the kitchen, family style with all the serving dishes on the table, or buffet style.

• Pie crusts can be made up to three weeks ahead of time and frozen until ready to use. Just line pie pan with dough and freeze, then thaw and bake later.

Whipped Sweet Potato Bake

6 medium sweet potatoes

½ cup packed brown sugar

½ cup half-and-half

¼ cup butter

1½ cups miniature marshmallows

Peel and cook potatoes in boiling water until tender; drain. Add brown sugar, half-and-half, and butter. Whip with an electric mixer on medium speed until fluffy. Place in a lightly greased 2½-quart baking dish.

Smooth top of sweet potato mixture; place marshmallows uniformly over the top, covering completely. Bake uncovered at 400° for about 10 to 12 minutes or until marshmallows are golden brown. Let stand 10 minutes before serving. Makes 10 to 12 servings.

Old-Fashioned Mashed Potatoes

See recipe on page 82.

Old-Fashioned Gravy

¾ cup cold water

2 tablespoons cornstarch

2 tablespoons all-purpose flour

drippings from turkey

2 cups hot water

salt and pepper

In a medium bowl, combine the cold water, cornstarch, and flour; mix until smooth. Set aside. Remove turkey from the roasting pan. Strain the drippings into a medium saucepan. Add the hot water and bring to a boil. Add flour mixture slowly, stirring constantly, until gravy reaches desired thickness. Add salt and pepper to taste.

Cranberry Orange Relish

Mix together cranberries and sugar; place in a lightly greased 2-quart baking dish. Cover and bake at 350° for 1 hour. Remove from oven, and stir in orange marmalade, orange, lemon juice, lemon peel, orange peel, and nuts. Mix well and refrigerate. Makes 8 to 10 servings.

4½ cups cranberries

1½ cups sugar

1 cup orange marmalade

1 fresh orange, peeled and diced

1 tablespoon. fresh lemon juice

1 teaspoon lemon peel, grated

2 teaspoons orange peel, grated

1 cup walnuts, chopped

Cranberry Raspberry Chutney

In a saucepan, combine cranberries, raspberries, raisins, and onion. Warm over medium heat. Add remaining ingredients and bring to a boil. Reduce heat and cook, uncovered, for 40 to 45 minutes, stirring occasionally. Refrigerate; serve cold. Makes 3 cups.

3 cups frozen cranberries

1 cup frozen raspberries

1 cup raisins

1 cup onion, chopped

¾ cup packed brown sugar

⅓ cup cider vinegar

1 clove garlic, minced

¼ teaspoon ground mustard

2 teaspoons mustard seed

2 teaspoons celery seed

¼ teaspoon ground ginger

¼ teaspoon allspice

¼ teaspoon cinnamon

1 turkey (18 to 20 pounds)

1 recipe pecan corn bread stuffing

3 tablespoons salt

1½ teaspoons pepper

¾ teaspoon poultry seasoning

4 tablespoons butter, softened

1 cup water

Roast Turkey

Make pecan corn bread stuffing (see recipe on page 103) and set aside.

Remove the giblets and neck bone from the turkey cavity. Release drumsticks from the metal clamps. Rinse with cold water inside and out. Pat the bird dry with paper towels.

In a small bowl, make a mixture of salt, pepper, and poultry seasoning. Sprinkle the neck and main cavity with mixture. With breast side down, loosely stuff the neck cavity with 1½ to 2 cups stuffing. Pull the neck skin over the stuffed area and fasten with skewers to the back of the turkey. With the breast side up, lightly stuff the main cavity with about 7 cups stuffing. Cover the exposed stuffing with foil. Replace drumsticks back together in metal clamps. (If there are no metal clamps, tie the drumsticks together with kitchen twine.)

Rub butter over the skin. Place the turkey, breast side up, on a metal rack in a roasting pan. Put in the lower half of the oven for about 4 hours at 350°. When the turkey is golden brown, add the 1 cup water and cover with an aluminum foil tent to prevent the turkey from getting too brown. To test for doneness, place a meat thermometer into the thickest part of the thigh, without touching the bone. The turkey is done when the thermometer reaches 180°.

Carefully remove roasting pan from oven. Lift out metal rack with turkey and let stand for 20 minutes before carving. Makes 12 to 14 servings.

DEFROSTING TIMES

Weight	In the Refrigerator	In Water
10 to 12 pounds	2 days	4 to 6 hours
12 to 14 pounds	3 days	6 to 9 hours
14 to 18 pounds	4 days	9 to 14 hours
18 pounds and over	4 to 5 days	14 to 24 hours

ROASTING TIMES

Weight	Unstuffed Turkey	Stuffed Turkey
10 to 12 pounds	1¾ to 2 hours	2 to 2¼ hours
12 to 14 pounds	2 to 2½ hours	2¼ to 3 hours
14 to 18 pounds	2½ to 3 hours	2¾ to 3½ hours
18 pounds and over	3½ hours +	4 hours +

Pecan Corn Bread Stuffing

Make corn bread recipe on page 55, doubling the recipe to make 2 loaves.

While corn bread cools, spread pecans on a baking sheet. Place in 425° oven for about 6 minutes. Set aside. Melt butter in skillet; sauté mushrooms, celery, and onions until tender. In large bowl, beat eggs; add parsley, raisins, soup, broth, poultry seasoning, and pepper. Add sautéed vegetables.

Sprinkle toasted pecans and crumbled corn bread over mixture. Toss.

Stuff seasoned turkey with stuffing and bake. Or, to bake pecan stuffing without stuffing the turkey, pour into a greased 9x13-inch baking dish. Bake uncovered at 350° for 40 to 45 minutes. Stuffing should be golden brown. Makes 12 to 14 servings.

1 cup pecans, toasted

4 tablespoons butter

2 cups fresh mushrooms, chopped

1 cup celery, chopped

½ cup onion, chopped

3 eggs

½ cup fresh parsley, chopped

½ cup dark raisins

1 10¾-ounce can condensed cream of chicken soup

2 14½-ounce cans chicken broth

1 teaspoon poultry seasoning

¼ teaspoon pepper

Roast Turkey

Sliced Roast Turkey with Cranberry Orange Relish, Pecan Corn Bread Stuffing, and Old-Fashioned Mashed Potatoes and Gravy

Pumpkin Pie

Put pumpkin in a large mixing bowl. In a separate bowl, mix together cinnamon, nutmeg, ginger, allspice, granulated sugar, brown sugar, salt, and cornstarch. Add to the pumpkin, and mix until blended. Add eggs and evaporated milk and mix until incorporated. Add water and mix well. Pour into an unbaked pie shell and bake at 375° for 50 to 60 minutes, or until a knife inserted in the center comes out clean. When cooled, top with whipped cream, if desired. Makes 1 pie.

pastry for 1-crust pie

1½ cups canned pumpkin

½ teaspoon cinnamon

½ teaspoon nutmeg

¼ teaspoon ground ginger

¼ teaspoon allspice

½ cup granulated sugar

⅓ cup brown sugar

1 teaspoon salt

1½ tablespoons cornstarch

2 eggs

1 cup evaporated milk

1 cup water

whipped cream (optional)

Raisin Cream Pie

Rinse and drain raisins. Put in saucepan, add water, and boil slowly for 10 minutes. Blend sugar, cornstarch, and salt. Add to raisin mixture and cook, stirring constantly, until clear and thick. Remove from heat and stir in vanilla, butter, and cream. Pour into pastry-lined pie pan and cover with top pastry. Flute edges and cut slits in top. Bake at 400° for 30 minutes or until pastry is light brown. Serve warm or cold. Makes 1 pie.

pastry for 2-crust pie

1 cup seedless raisins

1½ cups water

¾ cup sugar

3 tablespoons cornstarch

¼ teaspoon salt

1 teaspoon vanilla

1 tablespoon butter

1 cup light cream

Lion House Dinner Rolls

See recipe on page 57.

2 pounds fresh green beans*

3 tablespoons butter

¼ teaspoon onion powder

I clove garlic, peeled and crushed

seasoned salt to taste

Fresh String Green Beans

Break ends from beans. Beans should snap when broken; break in thirds. Place in vegetable steamer over boiling water, or cook in pot of boiling water, until tender, about 5 to 6 minutes. Drain and place in serving dish. Melt butter; stir in onion powder and crushed garlic. Toss seasoned butter with green beans. Season to taste with your favorite seasoned salt. Makes 6 to 8 servings.

* Frozen green beans are an option. Follow package instructions to cook beans. Then drain beans, and continue following recipe.

2 cups tart apples, cubed

2 cups celery, thinly sliced

½ cup red onion, chopped

I cup seedless red grapes

I cup green grapes

I cup miniature marshmallows

⅓ cup cold evaporated milk

½ teaspoon sugar

¼ teaspoon vanilla

3 tablespoons mayonnaise

3 tablespoons peanut butter

½ cup pecans (optional)

Crunchy Apple Salad

In large bowl, combine apples, celery, onion, grapes, and marshmallows. In a mixing bowl, beat evaoprated milk until frothy. Add sugar and vanilla; mix well. Add mayonnaise and peanut butter. Stir until smooth. Pour over apple mixture and toss until coated. Cover and refrigerate. Just before serving, stir in pecans, if desired. Makes 12 to 14 servings.

Candied Yam Soufflé

To make soufflé, boil, peel, and mash yams. In a large mixing bowl, beat together yams, milk, sugar, eggs, lemon juice, butter, and vanilla. Pour into casserole dish.

To make topping, mix together butter, brown sugar, flour, and pecans. Mix well. Spread on top of yam mixture. Bake at 350° for 30 to 40 minutes. Remove from oven and top with miniature marshmallows. Return to oven and bake for an additional 5 to 10 minutes, or until marshmallows are golden brown. Makes 10 to 12 servings.

SOUFFLÉ

6 medium yams

⅓ cup milk

¾ cup sugar

2 eggs

1 tablespoon lemon juice

½ cup butter

1 teaspoon vanilla

TOPPING

½ cup butter

1 cup brown sugar

¼ cup all-purpose flour

1 cup pecans, chopped

1½ cups miniature marshmallows

Oven-Baked Mashed Potatoes

Cook potatoes in boiling, salted water until tender; drain. Mash down and transfer to large bowl. Add half-and-half, salt, and butter. Beat with an electric mixer until light and fluffy. Fold in beaten eggs, sour cream, cottage cheese, and onions. Place in 3-quart baking dish.

In a medium bowl, mix crushed cracker crumbs with butter; sprinkle over top of potatoes. Bake, uncovered, at 350° for 30 to 35 minutes. Crumbs should be lightly browned. Makes 12 to 14 servings.

POTATOES

8 large potatoes, peeled and quartered

½ cup half-and-half

¾ teaspoon salt

2 tablespoons butter, melted

2 eggs, beaten

2 cups sour cream

2 cups small-curd cottage cheese

½ cup onion, chopped

TOPPING

1 cup butter-flavored crackers, crushed

2 tablespoons butter, melted

PORK ROAST

trimmed crown pork roast, with
bones cleaned

4 tablespoons butter

1 yellow onion, thinly sliced

1 carrot, thinly sliced

1 clove garlic

SALT MARINADE
(per pound of meat)

2 teaspoons kosher salt

½ teaspoon freshly ground black
pepper

½ teaspoon sage

½ teaspoon thyme

½ teaspoon crushed bay leaf

pinch allspice

2 cloves garlic, mashed

GRAVY

1 cup white grape juice

4 tablespoons onion, finely chopped

3 tablespoons butter

½ cup heavy cream

salt and pepper to taste

Crown Roast of Pork

Contact your butcher in advance to order a trimmed crown pork roast with the bones cleaned.

The day before serving, make the salt marinade by combining salt, pepper, sage, thyme, bay leaf, allspice and garlic. (Remember one recipe of salt marinade per pound of meat.) Rub the salt marinade well into the meat, then place meat in a large covered bowl in the refrigerator. Turn every 3 hours.

The next day, prepare 1 recipe of roasted cashew stuffing according to directions (see recipe on page 109). Set aside.

Preheat oven to 350°. Rub all the marinade off the meat and pat dry with paper towels. Put butter, onion, carrots, and garlic in the roasting pan. Place pan on the stove and heat over medium-high heat to sauté vegetables until soft, about 10 minutes. Put the roast in the pan. Fill center of the roast with roasted cashew stuffing. Cover and place in preheated oven. Bake for 15 minutes. Reduce heat to 325° and continue roasting, allowing 30 minutes per pound of meat.

Roast should be done when a meat thermometer registers at 160°. Transfer roast to a heated platter.

To make the gravy, add the grape juice, onion, and butter to the pan juices after removing roast. Boil the mixture down to ⅓ its original quantity; whisk to incorporate the drippings. Add the heavy cream, and heat without boiling. Season with salt and pepper to taste. Strain into a gravy bowl.

Makes 6 to 8 servings, depending on size of roast.

Roasted Cashew Stuffing

Place bread cubes in a single layer on an ungreased baking sheet. Bake at 225° for 30 to 40 minutes, tossing occasionally, until partially dried.

Meanwhile, combine the raisins and apple juice in a saucepan; bring to boil. Remove from heat; let stand 15 minutes. In large skillet, sauté celery, onion, garlic, and mushrooms in olive oil until tender. Add parsley, salt, sage, thyme, and pepper; mix well. Remove from heat.

Beat egg and broth in a bowl; add to vegetable mixture. Add bread cubes and raisin mixture; mix in cashews last. Toss well.

Use stuffing to stuff poultry or meat. Or, transfer to a greased 9x13-inch baking dish. Cover and bake at 325° for 30 minutes. Uncover and bake an additional 20 to 25 minutes or until lightly browned. Makes 10 to 12 servings.

8 cups day-old bread cubes

¾ cup raisins

½ cup apple juice

4 celery ribs, diced

1 large onion, chopped

3 cloves garlic, minced

1 cup fresh mushrooms, sliced

¼ cup olive oil

1 cup fresh parsley, minced

1 teaspoon salt

1½ teaspoons rubbed sage

¾ teaspoon dried thyme

¼ teaspoon pepper

1 egg

1½ to 2 cups chicken broth

1½ cups salted, roasted cashew pieces

Tips and Ideas

- Plan activities for children on the day of a holiday dinner. Games, crafts, or a nature walk will keep children entertained with minimal supervision. This allows parents time to work in the kitchen without constant interruption before the meal, as well as time to relax and visit after the meal.

- Start a new holiday tradition. Hide an almond in a special dessert and give a prize to the one who finds the nut in his or her serving. Have a drawing for the centerpiece. Make a fancy gingerbread house to decorate the table, and let the kids eat it for dessert. There are endless possibilities for new traditions; ask friends and neighbors what they do and be creative.

PUDDING

2½ cups all-purpose flour

1½ cups granulated sugar

2½ teaspoons nutmeg

½ teaspoon cloves

1 teaspoon salt

2½ teaspoons cinnamon

2½ teaspoons baking soda

1¼ cups brown sugar

2½ cups apples, grated

2½ cups carrots, grated

2½ cups potatoes, grated

2½ cups seedless raisins

1⅓ cups dates, chopped

1 cup maraschino cherries, chopped

1¾ cups butter, melted

1⅓ cups nuts, chopped

BUTTERSCOTCH SAUCE

1½ cups brown sugar

⅔ cup light corn syrup

½ cup water

dash salt

⅔ cup evaporated milk

In a large mixing bowl, measure flour, granulated sugar, nutmeg, cloves, salt, cinnamon, and soda. Mix together so that the spices are well distributed. Add to this mixture the brown sugar, apples, carrots, potatoes, raisins, dates, cherries, butter, and nuts. Mix on low speed until well blended.

Put mixture into 7 wide-mouth pint jars* that have been sprayed with non-stick spray. Cover the top of each jar with 2 layers of plastic wrap. Then cover with a piece of foil and put a rubber band around the foil. Steam for 4 hours. When pudding is done, refrigerate until cool. Take off plastic wrap and foil. Clean edges of jars and put on new plastic, foil, and rubber bands. Pudding will keep for months if it is kept cold. Serve with butterscotch sauce, if desired. Makes 30 servings pudding.

To make butterscotch sauce, combine brown sugar, corn syrup, water, and salt in a small saucepan. Heat to boiling, stirring until sugar is dissolved. Continue cooking until a small amount dropped in cold water forms a very soft ball. Remove from heat. Cool slightly, then stir in evaporated milk. Makes 2 cups sauce.

* *Different size cans or containers may be used as desired, as long as they are sprayed with non-stick spray.*

Christmas Pudding

Clockwise from Left: Red Carpet Cake, Luscious Lemon Cake, Pumpkin Cake, Meltdown Chocolate Cake*, and Yvoni's Pineapple Cake

* From the Formal Dinners chapter

10

Few can resist a glorious selection of mouth-watering desserts. Served buffet style, desserts can be a graceful way to entertain on a large scale. Some desserts can be made well ahead of time, and they make a spectacular presentation on any table. For the ultimate special occasion, set up a beautiful buffet table with flowers, silver, and crystal. For most events, however, the desserts themselves will look so exquisite that very little additional decorating will be necessary.

Luscious Lemon Cake
Lemon-Lime Cake
Yvoni's Pineapple Cake
Moon Cake
Pineapple Carrot Cake
Red Carpet Cake
Banana Split Cake
Chunky Chocolate Peanut Cake
Cherry Pineapple Cake
Pumpkin Cake
Fruity Cake
Cherry Chocolate Cake
Midnight Chocolate Cake

~

Caramel Apple Squares
German Chocolate Bars
Picnic Brownies
Chocolate Chip Cookies
Frosted Peanut Butter Bars
Filled Cookies
Sour Cream Raisin Bars
Fudge Nut Bars
Saucepan Bars
Poor Man's Bars

~

Lion House Pie Dough
Carmel Chocolate Pecan Pie
Cheesy Apricot Pie
Almond Chocolate Pie
Danish Kringle
Apple Kuchon
Cherry Cheese Tart
Chocolate Granite Cheesecake
Mississippi Mud

Luscious Lemon Cake

1 cup all-purpose flour

½ teaspoon salt

1 teaspoon baking powder

3 egg yolks

1 cup sugar, divided

1 tablespoon water

2 tablespoons lemon juice

1½ teaspoon lemon rind, grated

1½ teaspoons vanilla

3 egg whites

1 to 2 cups canned lemon pie filling

powdered sugar

Combine flour, salt, and baking powder and set aside. In a medium bowl, beat egg yolks and ½ cup of sugar until thick and lemon colored. In a separate bowl, mix together water, lemon juice, lemon rind, and vanilla; add this alternately with the flour mixture to the egg yolk mixture. Mix until smooth.

In a separate bowl, beat egg whites until soft peaks form. Gradually add remaining ½ cup of sugar and beat until stiff peaks form. Slowly pour the lemon mixture into the egg white mixture, folding together while you pour. Gently pour the batter into an ungreased 9-inch bundt cake pan.

Bake at 350° for 25 to 30 minutes, or until toothpick inserted into the center of cake comes out clean. Place cake upside down to cool. When cool, remove cake from pan and cut in half horizontally. Spread bottom half of cake with lemon pie filling and replace top half. Dust with powdered sugar. Makes 10 servings.

Lemon - Lime Cake

1 lemon cake mix*

1 3-ounce package lime gelatin*

1½ cups water

1 3-ounce package vanilla instant pudding mix

1 cup milk

1 8-ounce carton frozen whipped topping

Mix and bake cake according to high altitude directions on package. While cake is baking, dissolve gelatin in 1 cup boiling water, then add ½ cup cold water. Set aside until cake is done. Do not refrigerate.

When cake is done, remove from oven and poke holes in hot cake with a meat fork. Slowly pour gelatin over top of cake so it will go down in the holes. Refrigerate cake.

Blend pudding mix with 1 cup milk, using a wire whisk until it starts to thicken. Fold in whipped topping and spread on cooled cake. This cake needs to be kept refrigerated. Makes 12 servings.

* A wide variety of cakes can be made by changing the flavor of cake mix and gelatin.

Yvoni's Pineapple Cake

Preheat oven to 350°. Grease and flour a 9x13-inch cake pan.* Set aside. In a large mixing bowl, combine all ingredients except crushed pineapple. Blend well, then fold in pineapple. Place in prepared pan and bake for 40 to 50 minutes. Remove from oven and cool on rack. Makes about 15 servings.

Cake may be baked in any shape pan, such as a bundt cake pan or an angel food cake pan.

1 yellow pudding-in-the-mix cake mix

½ cup cream of coconut

½ cup pineapple juice

4 eggs

⅓ cup oil

½ to ¾ cup crushed pineapple, drained

Moon Cake

Preheat oven to 400°. In a small saucepan, mix the water and margarine. Bring to a boil. Add the flour all at once and stir rapidly until the mixture forms a ball. Remove from heat and cool.

With a wooden spoon or electric mixer, beat in the eggs, one at a time, beating well after each addition. Spread dough on an 11x15-inch ungreased cookie sheet. Bake for 30 minutes. Cool. (Crust will look like the moon's surface, which is how it gets its name.) Don't prick, let stand as is.

Beat the cream cheese until it is very soft. In another bowl, mix the milk and pudding mix. Blend cream cheese with pudding and mix together until smooth. Spread on crust; refrigerate 20 minutes.

Generously top with whipped topping. Drizzle with chocolate sauce and sprinkle with chopped nuts. Makes 20 servings.

Whipping cream may be substituted.

1 cup water

½ cup margarine

1 cup all-purpose flour

4 eggs

1 8-ounce package cream cheese

3½ cups milk

5 3-ounce packages vanilla instant pudding mix

1 12-ounce carton whipped topping, thawed*

¼ cup chocolate sauce

½ cup nuts, chopped

CAKE

1¾ cups sugar

1¼ cups oil

4 eggs

2¼ cups all-purpose flour

1 teaspoon baking soda

1 teaspoon salt

1 teaspoon cinnamon

¾ cup crushed pineapple, drained

3 cups carrots, grated

1 cup chopped nuts

1 cup raisins (optional)

½ cup chopped nuts for garnish (optional)

CREAM CHEESE ICING

1 pound powdered sugar

1 8-ounce package cream cheese, softened

½ cup butter or margarine, softened

2 teaspoons vanilla

Pineapple Carrot Cake

Preheat oven to 375°. Grease and flour a 9x13-inch baking pan. (If baked in a glass baking pan, set oven at 350°.)

Combine sugar, oil, and eggs; mix well. Sift together flour, soda, salt, and cinnamon; add to the first mixture. Add pineapple and continue mixing. Stir in carrots, nuts, and raisins.

Pour into prepared pan and bake for 40 minutes or until done. When cool, ice with cream cheese icing. This cake is better if baked a day or two ahead. Makes 15 servings.

To make icing, combine powdered sugar, cream cheese, butter, and vanilla and beat until light and fluffy. Frost cake and sprinkle with nuts, if desired.

Pineapple Carrot Cake

Red Carpet Cake

Preheat oven to 350°. Grease and lightly flour two 9-inch round cake pans.

In a large bowl, cream shortening, sugar, and eggs. Make a paste of the coloring and cocoa; add to the sugar mixture and blend. In a medium bowl, mix the salt and the soda with the flour. In a separate bowl, mix the buttermilk, vinegar, and vanilla together. Add the flour mixture and the buttermilk mixture alternately to the creamed mixture. Mix until blended.

Divide batter evenly between the two prepared pans and bake approximately 30 minutes. Overbaking will cause the cakes to be very dry. Cool layers. Cut each layer in half horizontally. You will have four layers.

To make the frosting, combine the milk and flour in a small saucepan; mix well. Cook over medium heat, stirring constantly until thick. Cover and let cool. Cream butter, sugar, and vanilla until fluffy. Add the cooled flour mixture and beat until fluffy; this will take approximately 5 minutes. When frosting is done, you should not be able to feel the sugar granules.

Assemble the cake by placing a layer of cake on a serving platter and spreading with a layer of baker's frosting. Add the next layer of cake and repeat until you end with the last layer of cake. Frost top and sides of cake with frosting. Makes 12 servings.

* Do not substitute margarine.

CAKE

⅔ cup shortening

1½ cups sugar

2 eggs

2 ounces or ¼ cup red food coloring

4 tablespoons cocoa powder

1 teaspoon salt

1 teaspoon baking soda

2¼ cups all-purpose flour

1 cup buttermilk

2 teaspoons vinegar

1 teaspoon vanilla

BAKER'S FROSTING

1½ cups milk

4½ tablespoons all-purpose flour

1½ cups butter*

1½ cups sugar

1 tablespoon vanilla

Tips and Ideas

• Cut desserts into small portions so guests can sample many different kinds.

• Use a variety of serving dishes in different sizes and heights. An odd-shaped or odd-sized dish will make a more interesting presentation than a standard platter.

CRUST

2 cups graham cracker crumbs

½ cup margarine, melted

FILLING

2 eggs

2 cups powdered sugar

¾ cup margarine, soft

TOPPING

4 large bananas

1 20-ounce can crushed pineapple, drained

1 12-ounce carton frozen whipped topping, thawed

1 bottle fudge topping

¼ cup nuts, chopped

¼ cup maraschino cherries, quartered

Banana Split Cake

To make the crust, mix together graham cracker crumbs and margarine; press in the bottom of an ungreased 9x13-inch pan. Refrigerate 10 to 12 minutes.

In a large bowl, beat together eggs, powdered sugar, and margarine until light and fluffy, approximately 10 to 12 minutes. Spread filling on top of crumb mixture.

Slice the bananas on top of the filling, then spread the pineapple on top of the bananas. Spread whipped topping on top of the pineapple. Heat the fudge topping slightly, then drizzle on top of the whipped topping. Cool. Garnish the top with chopped nuts and cherries.

Refrigerate overnight for best results. This dessert is very rich. Makes 15 servings.

Tips and Ideas

- To frost a layered cake, trim off any overhang from the top of each layer with a small serrated knife. Brush off any loose crumbs from the top and side. Next, apply frosting to the top of the first layer, and then apply it to the sides. Add the next layer and repeat. After frosting the entire cake, dip a flat metal spatula into hot water and use it to smooth the frosting before applying any decoration.

- Always include a beverage with a dessert buffet. Sweets tend to make guests thirsty, so it is also a good idea to have plenty of ice water on hand.

- Buy the best quality chocolate available. The richest chocolate contains the highest percentage of cocoa solids, so look for more than 60 percent cocoa content.

- Try garnishing with an ingredient from the dessert. For instance, chocolate curls or shavings, cinnamon sticks, a bed of golden toasted coconut, or a chocolate-dipped strawberry will add appeal to the dessert and flare to your serving table.

Chunky Chocolate Peanut Cake

Preheat oven to 350°. Grease two 9-inch round cake pans; dust with flour and tap out excess.

In a large mixing bowl, sift together flour, cocoa, baking powder, and salt. In a separate bowl, beat together brown sugar, peanut butter, and butter at medium speed until light and fluffy. Add eggs, one at a time, beating well after each egg. Stir in vanilla.

At low speed, alternately beat flour mixture and milk into peanut butter batter. Pour batter into prepared pans; smooth tops. Bake about 50 to 55 minutes, or until tops spring back when lightly pressed or toothpicks inserted in the centers come out clean. Transfer pans to cooling rack for 10 minutes. Turn cakes out onto racks to cool completely.

To prepare icing, beat together peanut butter, honey, powdered sugar, and cream cheese at medium speed until blended and smooth. Reserve about one cup of the icing. Place one cake layer on a serving plate. Spread top with one-quarter of remaining icing. Top with second layer of cake and spread remaining icing on top and sides of cake. Using a pastry bag fitted with a star tip, make a border around the top and bottom edge of cake with reserved icing. Sprinkle peanuts on top. Makes 12 servings.

CAKE

2 cups all-purpose flour

⅓ cup unsweetened cocoa powder, sifted

2 teaspoons baking powder

¼ teaspoon salt

2 cups brown sugar, firmly packed

1 cup chunky peanut butter, at room temperature

⅔ cup butter, softened

4 large eggs

2 teaspoons vanilla

¾ cup milk

½ cup peanuts, chopped, for garnish

ICING

1½ cups chunky peanut butter, at room temperature

¾ cup honey, at room temperature

⅔ cup powdered sugar

6 tablespoons cream cheese, softened

Cherry Pineapple Cake

1 21-ounce can cherry pie filling

1 20-ounce can crushed pineapple

1 package yellow or white cake mix

¾ cup butter

whipped topping or ice cream, if desired

Preheat oven to 350°. Grease a 9x13-inch pan. Dump pie filling in the bottom of pan and spread as evenly as possible. Dump crushed pineapple, juice and all, evenly over pie filling. Sprinkle cake mix evenly over the fruit. Do not stir.

Slice butter thinly and place pieces on top of mix, or melt butter and drizzle over top of cake mix, covering as much as possible. Do not stir or mix. Bake 45 minutes. Serve with whipped topping or ice cream. Makes 12 servings.

Pumpkin Cake

CAKE

2 cups all-purpose flour

2 teaspoons baking soda

½ teaspoon salt

1 teaspoon cloves

2 teaspoons cinnamon

½ teaspoon ginger

¼ teaspoon nutmeg

4 eggs

2 cups sugar

1 cup oil

1 16-ounce can pumpkin

chopped nuts, for garnish

CREAM CHEESE FROSTING

1 pound powdered sugar

1 8-ounce package cream cheese, softened

1 cup margarine, softened

2 teaspoons vanilla

Preheat oven to 350°. Grease and flour a 9x13-inch cake pan or two 9-inch round cake pans.

Sift flour with soda, salt, cloves, cinnamon, ginger, and nutmeg. Set aside. Beat eggs with sugar until light and fluffy. Beat in oil and pumpkin to blend. Add flour mixture and blend well. Bake for 1 hour or until toothpick inserted in the center comes out clean. Frost with cream cheese frosting.

To make frosting, beat together powdered sugar, cream cheese, margarine, and vanilla until fluffy. Spread on cake; garnish by sprinkling the top with chopped nuts. Makes 15 servings.

Fruity Cake

Preheat oven to 350°. Grease a 9-inch springform pan or a 9x13-inch oblong pan. Dust with flour; tap out excess.

Beat together butter and sugar until light and fluffy. Add eggs, one at a time, beating well after each addition. Set aside. Toss drained fruit cocktail with 1 tablespoon of the flour. Mix together remaining flour and baking powder.

At low speed, beat flour mixture into butter mixture until well combined. Fold in fruit. Spoon batter into prepared pan and smooth top.

Bake cake until golden brown and a toothpick inserted in the center comes out clean, approximately 45 to 50 minutes. Transfer pan to a wire rack to cool for 20 minutes. Remove sides of pan; cool completely on rack.

To make topping, combine evaporated milk, margarine, and sugar in a small saucepan. Cook for 2 minutes. Pour over cake and sprinkle with toasted coconut. Makes 12 servings.

CAKE

⅔ cup butter, softened

¾ cup granulated sugar

3 large eggs

1 14-ounce can fruit cocktail, drained

1½ cups all-purpose flour

1½ teaspoons baking powder

TOPPING

½ cup evaporated milk

½ cup margarine

¾ cup sugar

½ cup coconut, toasted

Cherry Chocolate Cake

Preheat oven to 350°. In a large bowl, carefully fold cake mix, eggs, and pie filling together by hand until well blended. Pour into a greased and floured 9x13-inch pan. Bake for 35 to 40 minutes.

To make chocolate icing, combine chocolate chips and milk in a saucepan and heat over low heat until chips are melted. Remove from heat, stir in butter, vanilla, and powdered sugar.

When cake is cool, frost with chocolate icing or thawed frozen whipped topping, if desired. Makes 15 servings.

CAKE

1 chocolate cake mix

3 eggs

1 21-ounce can cherry pie filling

frozen whipped topping (optional)

CHOCOLATE ICING

1¼ cups chocolate chips

⅓ cup evaporated milk

2 tablespoons butter

1 teaspoon vanilla

½ cup powdered sugar

Midnight Chocolate Cake

1½ cups all-purpose flour

¾ cup whole wheat flour

1 teaspoon baking soda

½ teaspoon baking powder

½ teaspoon cinnamon

½ teaspoon salt

4 ounces (4 squares) semi-sweet chocolate, coarsely chopped

1 ounce (1 square) unsweetened chocolate, coarsely chopped

½ cup boiling water

1 cup butter, softened

2 cups dark brown sugar, firmly packed

2 large eggs

¾ teaspoon vanilla

1 cup milk

powdered sugar

Preheat oven to 350°. Grease a 10-inch bundt cake pan. Dust with flour, and tap out excess.

In a large bowl, mix together flour, wheat flour, baking soda, baking powder, cinnamon, and salt. Mix coarsely chopped chocolate in boiling water until chocolate melts. Stir until smooth.

In another bowl, beat together butter and brown sugar at medium speed until light and fluffy. Beat in eggs, one at a time, beating well after each addition. Beat in vanilla.

At low speed, alternately add flour mixture and milk to butter mixture. Beat in chocolate mixture until combined. Pour batter evenly into prepared pan. Bake cake until a toothpick inserted near the center comes out clean, about 40 to 45 minutes. Transfer pan to wire rack to cool for 10 minutes. Turn out and dust with powdered sugar. Makes 12 servings.

Caramel Apple Squares

1¾ cups unsifted flour

1 cup quick cooking oatmeal

½ cup firmly packed brown sugar

½ teaspoon baking soda

½ teaspoon salt

1 cup butter, cold

1 cup walnuts, chopped

20 caramels, unwrapped

1 can sweetened condensed milk

1 21-ounce can apple pie filling

In a large bowl, combine the flour, oatmeal, brown sugar, baking soda, and salt. Cut in the butter until crumbly. Reserve 1½ cups of this crumb mixture; press the remaining mixture on the bottom of a 9x13-inch baking pan.

Bake at 375° for 15 minutes; remove from oven. Add the nuts to the reserved mixture and set aside.

In a heavy saucepan over low heat (or in a microwave-safe bowl) melt the caramels with the condensed milk, stirring until smooth. Spoon the apple filling over the baked crust. Top with the caramel mixture, then crumble the reserved crumb mixture over the top.

Bake 20 minutes or until set. Cool and cut into squares. This may be served warm with ice cream. Makes 24 squares.

Clockwise from Left: Poor Man's Bars, German Chocolate Bars, Fudge Nut Bars, Picnic Brownies, and Sour Cream Raisin Bars with Ice Cream and Berries

⅔ cup margarine or butter, softened

1 package German chocolate
cake mix

1 cup semi-sweet chocolate chips

1 tub coconut pecan
ready-to-spread frosting

¼ cup milk

4 ounces baking chocolate

1 cup butter

2 cups sugar

2 teaspoons vanilla

1 teaspoon salt

4 eggs

1¾ cups all-purpose flour

⅔ cup walnuts, pecans,
or almonds, chopped

1 cup chocolate chips

1¾ cups butter, softened

1¾ cups brown sugar

1¼ cups granulated sugar

4 eggs

5½ tablespoons water

1½ teaspoons vanilla

6 cups all-purpose flour

1½ teaspoons salt

1½ teaspoons baking soda

3 cups chocolate chips

German Chocolate Bars

Preheat oven to 350°. Lightly grease a 9x13-inch pan. In a medium bowl, cut margarine or butter into cake mix using pastry blender or fork. Press half of the mixture (about 2½ cups) in the bottom of the pan. Bake 10 minutes. Sprinkle chocolate chips over baked layer. Drop frosting by tablespoonfuls over chocolate chips. Stir milk into the remaining cake mixture and drop teaspoonfuls of this batter on top of frosting. Bake 25 to 30 minutes or until cake portions of the surface are slightly dry to the touch. Cool completely. Cut into 24 squares (4 rows by 6 rows). Cover and refrigerate. Makes 24 bars.

Picnic Brownies

Preheat oven to 350°. Grease two 9-inch round pans. In the top of a double boiler, or in a microwave safe bowl, melt the chocolate and butter. In a medium bowl, mix together sugar, vanilla, and salt; add to the melted chocolate mixture and blend well. Add eggs, one at a time, beating well after each addition. Add the flour and mix well.

Divide the batter equally into the prepared pans. Spread evenly and sprinkle the top of each with the chopped nuts and chocolate chips. Bake for 25 minutes. Do not over bake. Allow to cool completely before cutting. With a long knife (one that is longer than the brownies are wide), cut the brownies by pressing the knife straight down through the brownies; cut into 8 pie-shaped pieces. Makes 16 brownies.

Chocolate Chip Cookies

Preheat oven to 350°. Line a cookie sheet with wax paper; set aside. In a large mixing bowl, cream butter and sugars. Add eggs, water, and vanilla and mix until creamy. Mix together the flour, salt, and soda; add to the butter mixture. Mix well. Gently fold in chocolate chips, mixing only until chips are evenly distributed. (Overmixing results in broken chips and discolored dough.) Drop by teaspoonfuls onto prepared cookie sheet. Bake for 8 to 10 minutes or until golden brown. Makes 5 to 6 dozen 3½-inch cookies.

Frosted Peanut Butter Bars

Preheat oven to 350°. Grease a 9x13-inch cake pan and set aside.

In a large bowl, stir together butter and peanut butter until creamy. Gradually beat in sugars. Add eggs one at a time, beating well after each addition. Beat in vanilla.

In a separate bowl, mix together flour, baking powder, and salt. Mix flour mixture into peanut butter mixture. Spread into the prepared cake pan and bake for 22 to 25 minutes. Remove from oven and let cool.

To make frosting, beat together peanut butter and vanilla until creamy. Alternately beat in milk and powdered sugar. Beat mixture until fluffy and easy to spread. Spread on top of bars. Makes 20 bars.

BARS

½ cup butter

½ cup chunky peanut butter

½ cup sugar

½ cup brown sugar

3 eggs

1 teaspoon vanilla

2 cups all-purpose flour

2 teaspoons baking powder

¼ teaspoon salt

FROSTING

⅓ cup peanut butter

1 teaspoon vanilla

¼ cup milk

2½ cups powdered sugar

Filled Cookies

Preheat oven to 400°. Grease a cookie sheet. In a large bowl, cream shortening and sugar. Add eggs and beat well. Mix flour, cocoa, and salt together; add alternately to the first mixture with the sour milk. Combine soda and hot water; add to the dough. Drop by heaping tablespoonfuls onto greased cookie sheet. Bake 10 to 15 minutes. Cool, slice in half horizontally, and fill.

To make filling, mix vanilla, milk, powdered sugar, and shortening on low speed until well blended, then on high speed until fluffy. Spread desired amount between sliced cookies. Makes 4 dozen filled cookies.

COOKIES

1 cup shortening

1 cup sugar

2 eggs, beaten

5 cups all-purpose flour

¾ cup cocoa

1½ teaspoons salt

1½ cups sour milk

2 teaspoons baking soda

1 cup hot water

FILLING

2 tablespoons vanilla

4 tablespoons milk

4 cups powdered sugar

1 cup shortening

Sour Cream Raisin Bars

1¾ cups quick cooking oatmeal

1¾ cups all-purpose flour

1 cup brown sugar, firmly packed

1 teaspoon baking soda

1 cup butter, melted

4 egg yolks

1½ cups sugar

3 tablespoons cornstarch

2 cups sour cream

2 cups raisins

Preheat oven to 350°. In a large bowl, combine oatmeal, flour, brown sugar, and soda; blend well. Add butter and mix well. Pat ⅔ of the mixture into the bottom of a 9x13-inch pan. Bake 15 to 20 minutes. Cool.

Make the filling by combining the egg yokes, sugar, cornstarch, sour cream, and raisins in a medium saucepan. Bring mixture to a boil; reduce heat and simmer 5 to 10 minutes. Stir constantly to avoid burning. Pour hot mixture over baked layer. Crumble the remaining ⅓ of the oatmeal mixture over the top and bake for 15 to 20 minutes. Allow to cool before cutting. Makes 20 bars.

Fudge Nut Bars

BARS

1 cup margarine

2 cups brown sugar

2 eggs

2 teaspoons vanilla

2½ cups all-purpose flour

1 teaspoon baking soda

1 teaspoon salt

3 cups quick-cooking oats

FUDGE FILLING

1 12-ounce package semi-sweet chocolate chips

1 can sweetened condensed milk

2 tablespoons margarine

½ teaspoon salt

1 cup nuts, chopped

2 teaspoons vanilla

Preheat oven to 350°. Grease a 10x15-inch jelly-roll pan. In a large bowl, cream together margarine, brown sugar, eggs, and vanilla. Add the flour, soda, and salt; mix well. Blend in the oats. Set aside while you make the fudge filling.

In the top of a double boiler (or in the microwave in a glass dish), melt the chocolate chips together with the milk, margarine, and salt. Stir until smooth. Remove from heat; add nuts and vanilla.

Reserve ⅓ of the dough; spread the rest in the prepared pan. Cover with the fudge filling. Crumble the remaining dough on top of filling. Bake for 25 to 30 minutes. Allow to cool completely, then cut into bars. Makes 30 bars.

Saucepan Bars

Preheat oven to 350°. Grease and flour a 9x13-inch cake pan. In a medium saucepan, melt the butter. Remove from heat, and with a wooden spoon stir in the sugars, water, vanilla, and egg. Add the flour, baking powder, and salt; stir well. Add the chips, coconut, and nuts and mix until evenly distributed. Pour into prepared pan and spread out evenly. (It will seem fairly thin.) Bake for 20 to 25 minutes or until light golden brown. When cool, cut into bars. Makes 20 bars.

½ cup butter

½ cup brown sugar

½ cup granulated sugar

2 tablespoons water

1 teaspoon vanilla

1 egg

1 cup all-purpose flour

1¼ teaspoons baking powder

¼ teaspoon salt

1 cup chocolate or butterscotch chips

1 cup coconut

½ cup walnuts, chopped (optional)

Saucepan Bars, Cream Cheese Brownies, and Frosted Peanut Butter Bars

Poor Man's Bars

Preheat oven to 350°. Grease and flour a 10x15-inch or 12x17-inch jelly-roll pan. Place raisins and water in a small saucepan; boil until half the water is gone. Remove from heat and allow to cool while mixing the other ingredients.

In a large bowl, cream sugar and shortening; add egg and beat well. In a separate bowl, mix flour, salt, soda, cinnamon, and allspice. Add to the creamed mixture, stirring slightly. Add raisins and water; stir until mixed. Spread thinly on prepared pan. Bake 25 to 30 minutes. Allow to cool slightly before frosting.

To make frosting, mix together powdered sugar, half-and-half, and vanilla until smooth. Makes 36 bars.

* Cream or evaporated milk may be substituted.

BARS

1 cup raisins

2 cups water

1 cup sugar

½ cup shortening

1 egg

2 cups all-purpose flour

½ teaspoon salt

1 teaspoon soda

1 teaspoon cinnamon

1 teaspoon allspice

FROSTING

2 cups powdered sugar

2 to 3 tablespoons half-and-half*

1 teaspoon vanilla

Lion House Pie Dough

¼ cup butter

⅓ cup lard

¼ cup margarine

⅓ cup shortening

1 tablespoon sugar

½ teaspoon baking powder

1 teaspoon salt

1 tablespoon powdered
nonfat dry milk

1½ cups pastry flour*

1½ cups bread flour*

½ cup cold water**

Using a mixer, cream together butter, lard, margarine, and shortening. In a separate bowl, mix sugar, baking powder, salt, and powdered dry milk together, then add to the creamed butter mixture and mix briefly. Add pastry flour and beat until it is just blended. Add bread flour and mix slightly. Pour water in and beat again only until water is incorporated. Dough is easiest to handle if refrigerated for 30 minutes at this point.

Divide dough into two or three balls. Roll out on floured board. Line pie pan with dough, and cut off excess. Flute edges. Prick holes in bottom of dough with fork. Bake empty pie shell at 425° for 12 to 15 minutes or until light golden brown. Or fill pie and follow instructions for the particular pie recipe you are using. Makes 2 to 3 pie shells.

* 3 cups all-purpose flour may be used instead of the combination of bread and pastry flour. Mix slightly with mixer if using all-purpose flour.

** 1 tablespoon more water may be needed.

Caramel Chocolate Pecan Pie

unbaked 9-inch pie shell

1 cup pecan pieces

1 cup semi-sweet chocolate chips

½ cup caramel ice cream topping

1 8-ounce package cream cheese

1 cup dairy sour cream

½ cup sugar

1 teaspoon vanilla

3 eggs

cocoa powder to garnish

Preheat oven to 350°. In the unbaked pie shell, sprinkle the pecan pieces and chocolate chips. Drizzle the caramel topping over the top; set aside while you make the filling.

In a medium bowl, beat the cream cheese until soft. Add the sour cream, sugar, and vanilla and mix until smooth. Add the eggs, beating on low speed until just combined. Pour in the prepared crust. Bake approximately 45 minutes, until the center appears set. Cool, then chill at least 1 hour. Dust with cocoa powder. Makes 8 servings.

Cheesy Apricot Pie

Beat sugar and cream cheese together until fluffy and light. Beating on low speed, slowly pour in the cream. Blend in the vanilla and almond extract.

Drain the apricot halves, reserving the syrup. Place ½ cup of the syrup in a small saucepan; soften the gelatin in the syrup. Slightly heat this mixture to help the gelatin dissolve. Stir gelatin mixture into cream cheese mixture; pour into pie shell and chill 2 to 3 hours, or until set.

Arrange apricot halves on top of the cream filling in a decorative manner. Spoon the melted currant jelly over the apricots. Chill pie. Serve with whipped cream if desired. Makes 8 servings.

baked 9-inch pie shell or graham cracker crust

⅓ cup sugar

1 8-ounce package cream cheese

1¼ cups cream

1 teaspoon vanilla

¼ teaspoon almond extract

1 10½-ounce can apricot halves

1 envelope unflavored gelatin

½ cup currant jelly, melted

whipped cream, if desired

Almond Chocolate Pie

To toast the almonds, preheat oven to 350°. Place almonds on a cookie sheet and bake for 5 to 7 minutes. Almonds should be light golden brown. Remove from oven. Be careful not to overcook; almonds will continue to brown after being removed from the oven.

In the top of a double boiler, melt the chocolate bar, half-and-half, and marshmallows. In a large bowl, whip the cream until stiff; fold cream and almonds into chocolate mixture. Pour into crust and refrigerate to cool. When cool, place in freezer. Remove from freezer 1 hour before serving. Makes 8 servings.

baked 9-inch pie shell or graham cracker crust

½ cup almond slivers, toasted

1 7-ounce chocolate bar

½ cup half-and-half

18 large marshmallows

1 cup heavy whipping cream

DOUGH

1 cup all-purpose flour

½ cup butter

2 tablespoons water

TOPPING

½ cup butter

1 cup water

1 teaspoon almond extract

1 cup all-purpose flour

¼ teaspoon salt

3 eggs

sliced almonds, for garnish

GLAZE

2 cups powdered sugar

1 teaspoon almond extract

3 to 4 tablespoons cream,
half-and-half, or canned milk

Danish Kringle

Preheat oven to 350°. Place flour and butter in a mixing bowl and cut together until the size of small peas. Sprinkle with the water and mix together. Divide the dough into two equal parts; flatten into rectangles (about 4 inches wide and 15 inches long) on an ungreased cookie sheet. Make the rectangles as even as possible. Set aside while you make the topping.

Combine butter and water in a small saucepan and bring to a boil. Remove from heat and add almond extract, flour, and salt. Stir with a wooden spoon until the dough leaves the edge of the pan and forms a ball. Add one egg at a time, completely incorporating egg after each addition. (Use a wooden spoon or spatula to stir; do not use a mixer.) Divide in half and spread evenly on the 2 rectangles of dough. Bake for 50 minutes or until light brown. (The topping will rise unevenly.) Cool slightly, then drizzle powdered sugar glaze on top and sprinkle with sliced almonds.

To make glaze, mix together powdered sugar, almond extract, and cream. You may need to adjust the amount of cream depending on the brand of powdered sugar you use. (Glaze should run slowly through a fork when scooped up.)

Cut Danish kringle in slices about 1½ to 2 inches wide, depending on how many servings you need. This is a very light dessert. Makes 12 servings.

Tips and Ideas

- Use serving plates that are five to seven inches in diameter, and allow for more than one per guest.

- Garnish desserts and serving platters just before serving with edible flowers, such as rose petals or pansies, a wreath of nasturtiums, or crystallized violets.

Cherry Cheese Tart, Chocolate Granite Cheesecake, and Danish Kringle

Apple Kuchon

1 package yellow cake mix

½ cup butter, softened

1 21-ounce can apple pie filling

¼ cup sugar

1 teaspoon cinnamon

1 cup sour cream

1 egg

ice cream or whipped topping, if desired

Preheat oven to 350°. Place dry cake mix in a medium bowl and cut in butter as you would for pie dough. Pat mixture lightly into a 9x13-inch cake pan, building up the edges slightly. Bake for 10 minutes. Arrange apple filling over warm crust. Mix sugar and cinnamon together and sprinkle over filling. Blend the sour cream and egg, then drizzle over the top. Bake for 25 minutes. Serve warm or cold, plain or with ice cream or whipped topping. Makes 15 servings.

Cherry Cheese Tart

CRUST

1 cup graham cracker crumbs

2 tablespoons ground almonds

4 tablespoons butter or margarine, melted

FILLING

1 8-ounce package cream cheese

1 to 2 teaspoons honey

TOPPING

1 15-ounce can Bing cherries

2 teaspoons cornstarch

2 tablespoons apricot jelly

1 tablespoon lemon juice

Prepare crust by combining cracker crumbs, almonds, and butter. Mix together and press firmly into an 8-inch pie plate. Bake at 300° for 15 minutes. Set aside to cool.

Prepare filling by beating together cream cheese and honey. Spread evenly over crust. Drain cherries, reserving 8 tablespoons of the liquid. Cut cherries in half. Arrange, cut side down, on cheese layer.

Combine reserved cherry liquid and cornstarch in a small saucepan. Stir in jelly and lemon juice, mixing well. Bring to a boil over low heat, stirring constantly. Reduce heat and simmer 2 minutes longer or until thickened. Spoon hot glaze over cherries to cover completely. Chill 2 to 3 hours before serving. Makes 6 to 8 servings.

Chocolate Granite Cheesecake

Press cookie crumbs into the bottom of a 9-inch springform pan. Combine cream cheese, sugar, eggs, and vanilla in a large mixing bowl. Beat until smooth and fluffy. Pour half the cheese mixture into crumb-lined pan.

In the top of a double boiler (or in a glass microwave-safe bowl), melt 2 squares of the chocolate. Blend chocolate into remaining cheese mixture. Drizzle chocolate mixture over white mixture in pan, making swirls. Bake at 300° for 50 minutes or until set. Chill 2 hours.*

For the frosting, melt 6 squares of the chocolate; combine with sour cream. Spread over the chilled cheesecake. Serve immediately or refrigerate until ready to serve. Makes 12 servings.

Cheesecake may be frozen at this point until needed. Allow to thaw before frosting.

CRUST

2 cups chocolate sandwich cookie crumbs

FILLING

3 8-ounce packages cream cheese, at room temperature

1 cup sugar

5 eggs

1 teaspoon vanilla

2 ounces (2 squares) semi-sweet chocolate, melted

FROSTING

6 ounces (6 squares) semi-sweet chocolate, melted

½ cup sour cream

Mississippi Mud

Preheat oven to 350°. Grease and flour a 9x13-inch cake pan. Cream margarine and sugar together. Beat in cocoa and vanilla. Add eggs, one at a time, beating well after each addition. Blend in flour. Add nuts and mix lightly. Spread evenly in prepared pan and bake for 25 minutes.

Remove from oven and sprinkle the marshmallows on top while hot. Return to the oven for 3 more minutes. (Marshmallows will puff up.) Allow to cool for 1 hour, then frost.

To make frosting, place margarine, powdered sugar, cocoa, and milk in mixing bowl and start mixing on low speed. When ingredients are incorporated, turn speed to high and beat well. Spread on top of the marshmallows. Let set for about 12 hours, if possible, to allow the marshmallows to be cut more easily. Makes 20 servings.

CAKE

1 cup margarine

2 cups sugar

⅓ cup cocoa

2 tablespoons vanilla

4 eggs

1½ cups all-purpose flour

1½ cups nuts, chopped

1 pound miniature marshmallows

FROSTING

¼ cup margarine

1½ cups powdered sugar

⅓ cup cocoa

⅓ cup evaporated milk

Chicken Salad Pita, Grape Cluster, and Potato Chips

Children's Birthday Parties

11

Children's birthday parties can be some of the most memorable celebrations for the children and some of the most taxing for the hosts. Having the party some place other than the living room, such as the backyard, local park, or playground can minimize stress. You can keep the food simple without sacrificing quality. Pick a theme for your party; be creative and remember that easy-to-prepare, tasty dishes can be the centerpiece around which you can plan party games, activities, and decorations.

Safari Snake Sandwiches

Banana Pops

Jungle Juice

Tiger Paw Cupcakes

❧

Chuck Wagon Sloppy Joes

Corral Carrot Sticks

Root Beer

Wagon Wheel Ice Cream Sandwiches

❧

Chicken Salad Pitas

Potato Chips

Grape Cluster

Pink Flamingo Smoothies

S'mores Bars

Safari Snake Sandwiches

1 loaf unsliced French bread (about 16 inches long)

¼ cup mayonnaise

2 teaspoons prepared mustard

8 ¾-ounce slices American or Swiss cheese

8 slices cooked ham

At one-inch intervals, make 15 cuts across the bread loaf, being careful not to cut through the bottom crust. Mix the mayonnaise and mustard in a small bowl. Using a knife or spatula, spread the mustard mixture between *every other* opening in the loaf.

Preheat oven to 375°. Place one cheese slice on top of one ham slice and fold together to form a triangle. Insert triangles into openings in the bread that have been spread with the mustard mixture. Press bread loaf together and wrap in foil. Place on a cookie sheet and bake for 25 to 30 minutes or until hot.

To serve, carefully remove the foil. Cut through the bottom crusts of the unfilled openings in the bread loaf. Makes 8 sandwiches.

Banana Pops

BANANA POPS

8 whole bananas

8 wooden skewers

milk

TOPPINGS

granola

graham cracker crumbs

sliced almonds

chopped peanuts

flaked coconut

Peel bananas and discard peels. Insert a skewer lengthwise into each banana. Dip each banana in milk, then roll in any of the toppings. Place on wax paper to dry. Put bananas in freezer to partially freeze, if desired. Makes 8 pops.

Safari Snake Sandwich, Jungle Juice, Banana Pops, and Tiger Paw Cupcakes

Jungle Juice

Combine frozen juice concentrate, milk, water, sugar, and ice in blender and blend until smooth. Makes 8 servings.

2/3 cup frozen juice concentrate (any flavor)

1 cup milk

1 cup water

1/2 cup sugar

10 to 12 ice cubes

Tiger Paw Cupcakes

Put paper cupcake liners in cupcake pan. Preheat oven to 350°.

In a large mixing bowl, combine cake mix, water, oil, and eggs. Mix with an electric mixer until well blended. Fill each cupcake liner 1/4 to 1/3 full. Bake for 13 to 15 minutes.

In a small saucepan, combine flour, sugar, and milk. Heat over medium heat, stirring to remove lumps. Boil until mixture thickens.

Cool mixture, then add margarine, shortening, sugar, vanilla, and salt. Beat for about 5 minutes until fluffy. Fit decorator bag with a #4 or #5 tip. Insert tip in cupcake and squeeze in small amount of filling. Frost with remaining filling.

Decorate to resemble tiger paws by topping each cupcake with a small peppermint patty candy, then placing 3 chocolate chips, points up, around the edge of the cupcake. Makes 24 cupcakes.

CUPCAKES

1 package cake mix (any flavor)

1 cup hot water

1/3 cup vegetable oil

4 eggs

FILLING

1/3 cup all-purpose flour

1/3 cup sugar

1 cup milk

1/2 cup margarine

1/2 cup shortening

3/4 cup sugar

1 teaspoon vanilla

dash salt

24 peppermint patties

chocolate chips

2 pounds ground beef

1 8-ounce can tomato sauce or
1 10-ounce can chicken gumbo soup

½ cup chopped onion

¼ cup ketchup

2 tablespoon brown sugar

¼ teaspoon prepared mustard

8 to 10 hamburger buns, split

CRUNCHY COOKIES

1 cup butter or margarine, softened

1 cup granulated sugar

1 cup lightly packed brown sugar

2 eggs

2 teaspoons vanilla

1½ cups all-purpose flour

1 teaspoon baking powder

½ teaspoon baking soda

2 cups oatmeal

2 cups crispy rice cereal

1 cup coconut

ICE CREAM

½ gallon vanilla ice cream,
slightly softened

FROSTING

1 cup semi-sweet chocolate chips

2 tablespoons shortening

Chuck Wagon Sloppy Joes

Cook ground beef in 10-inch skillet over medium heat until brown; drain. Stir in tomato sauce or soup, onion, ketchup, brown sugar, and mustard. Simmer uncovered over low heat for 10 minutes, stirring occasionally. Heat oven to 325°. Wrap buns in foil and heat in oven for 15 minutes. Spoon meat mixture onto warm buns. Makes 8 to 10 servings.

Wagon Wheel Ice Cream Sandwiches

Make the cookies by creaming together the butter and sugars. Add eggs and vanilla. Stir in flour, baking powder, and soda. Add oatmeal, cereal, and coconut, and mix well. Drop by teaspoonfuls 2 inches apart on a greased cookie sheet. Bake at 350° for 10 minutes. Remove from cookie sheet immediately. Cool completely.

Line a cookie sheet with wax paper; place in freezer until chilled. To assemble ice cream sandwiches, lay one cookie bottom side up and spread on 1 slightly rounded tablespoon of vanilla ice cream. Top with another cookie, top side up. Press cookies together slightly. Place cookie on chilled cookie sheet. Repeat until all cookies are assembled, then place cookie sheet immediately back into freezer. Freeze 2 to 3 hours, or until firm.

Heat chocolate chips and shortening in small saucepan over medium heat, stirring occasionally, until chocolate is melted. Cool mixture for 2 minutes. Dip half of each frozen ice cream sandwich into chocolate mixture to coat. Place sandwiches back into freezer and freeze until chocolate is firm. Wrap sandwiches in plastic wrap and store in freezer until ready to serve. Makes 3 dozen cookie sandwiches.

Note: Cookies will be thin.

Chuck Wagon Sloppy Joe, Carrot Sticks, Wagon Wheel Ice Cream Sandwich, and Root Beer

2 cups cooked chicken, cubed

¾ cup celery, diced

¼ teaspoon salt

I cup seedless grapes

I 4-ounce package chopped cashews

I 16-ounce can chunk or crushed pineapple, drained

I cup whipped topping

½ cup mayonnaise

I teaspoon lemon juice

12 6-inch pita breads, halved

I pint strawberries

2 bananas

4 8-ounce containers raspberry yogurt

2 cups milk

Chicken Salad Pitas

Combine chicken, celery, salt, grapes, nuts, and pineapple in large bowl and mix well. In a separate smaller bowl, combine whipped topping, mayonnaise, and lemon juice and mix until fluffy. Fold dressing into chicken mixture.

Spoon about ⅓ cup of filling into each pita bread half. Makes 24 pita sandwiches.

Pink Flamingo Smoothies

Wash and hull strawberries. Peel the bananas and slice them into quarters. Place all fruit in blender. Spoon yogurt into blender and add milk. Cover and puree until all ingredients are thoroughly combined. Pour into glasses. Makes 8 shakes.

Tips and Ideas

• Give arriving children something to do as they are waiting for the party to begin.

• Plan more activities than you think you'll need. Let your child be involved in selecting and organizing the activities.

• Have children sit down to eat. This will help avoid choking and other injuries, and it will substantially cut down on the amount of crumbs and spills to clean up later.

• Instead of a traditional birthday cake, have children frost and decorate individual cupcakes with a creative assortment of sprinkles, small candies, coconut, and candles.

S'mores Bars

Thoroughly mix graham cracker crumbs, sugar, and butter together in a medium bowl. Press firmly into the bottom of a greased 9x13-inch pan; chill.

Prepare brownie mix according to package directions. Pour onto chilled graham cracker crust. Bake according to package directions.

Remove pan from oven and top evenly with marshmallows and chocolate chips. Return the pan to oven for 3 minutes. Cool before cutting into squares. Makes 16 bars.

1½ cups graham cracker crumbs, finely crushed

3 tablespoons sugar

6 tablespoons butter or margarine

1 package brownie mix

3 cups miniature marshmallows

1 cup semi-sweet chocolate chips

S'mores Bar

Tips and Ideas

• Let children design their own invitations using basic craft materials, such as colored paper, crayons, glitter, and stickers.

• Keep the party short. One or two hours is about all young children can manage.

• Stick to basics. Small children don't need circus clowns, magicians, and pony rides to enjoy themselves.

• To reduce the stress and cleanup required after hosting a group of children in your home, have your party outside. Parks, playgrounds, and backyards are great places for kids to have fun.